Wh... GOD

says GO

Discovery House Publishers

Books, music, and videos that feed the soul with the Word of God

Box 3566 Grand Rapids, MI 49501

When GOD says GO

The Amazing Journey

of a Slave's Daughter

Lorry Lutz

Discovery House Publishers is affiliated with RBC Ministries,
Grand Rapids, Michigan 49501.

Discovery House books are distributed to the trade exclusively
by Barbour Publishing, Inc., Uhrichsville, Ohio 44683.

Unless otherwise indicated, Scripture references are from
the *Holy Bible, New International Version* (NIV).

Library of Congress Cataloging-in-Publication Data

Lutz, Lorry
    [Born to lose, bound to win]
    When God says go : the amazing story of a slave's daughter
/ Lorry Lutz.
      p.   cm.
Originally published: Born to lose, bound to win. Irvine, CA:
Harvest House Publishers, 1980.
    ISBN 1-57293-098-5
    1. George, Eliza, 1879–1979. 2. Missionaries—Liberia—
Biography. 3. Missionaries—United States—Biography.
I. Title.
    BV3625.L6 G465 2002
266'.61'092—dc21   2002012276

Printed in the United States of America.

02 03 04 05 06 07 08 / DP / 7 6 5 4 3 2 1

To my beloved husband Allen who has encouraged
and prayed for me every step of the way

And to Allen Finley who never doubted
that this story must be told.

CONTENTS

FOREWORD
by Sherwood Eliot Wirt

Mother Eliza Davis George. What a beautiful person! To know her was to sense all over again the infinite capacity of the human spirit when touched by the Spirit of God.

A poor little black girl growing up in segregated Texas, she made the "mistake" of taking seriously the stories she learned in Sunday school. She literally wanted the world to know about Jesus and sought to be used of God to that end. When the religious establishment set out to correct her visionary ideas, she found that she had to choose between the "important" people and Jesus. She chose Jesus, went to Africa on a shoestring, and without any portfolio, any support agency beyond a few friends, any anything, she won her way. One by one the barriers of sex, color, status, and funding toppled before her. One woman with God proved more than America or Africa could deter.

She went to the heads of government and wheedled gifts of land out of them without a single influential person representing or sponsoring her.

She pulled a naked little boy out of the bush, put pants on him, and enrolled him in her school. Today he holds a graduate degree from the Golden Gate Seminary in California and a doctoral degree in Missions from the Reformed Theological Seminary in Mississippi. He was one of Liberia's notable Christian educators and statesmen.

She came back to Texas and raised money where there was no money to be raised. She sent every penny of it to Africa, and followed it to see that it was properly spent.

She lived to be a hundred, and when she died full of years, her faith in Jesus was as strong as ever.

Eliza Davis George. You will love her story as Lorry tells it so effectively in these pages. Eliza belongs with the heroes of the faith, one of God's quiet people who left the human race better than she found it. God rest her soul.

*N*ote: You may notice that many individuals are introduced in the story as Mr. or Mrs. That is because Mother Eliza and others interviewed for this book customarily referred to people deferentially, in the formal tradition. For many others only first names were customarily used.

Introduction

*A*s Mother Eliza George neared the century mark, Allen Finley, then president of CNEC (now known as Partners International) asked me to write her story. Allen had been working with Mother Eliza and her spiritual son, Gus Marwieh, for years, and knew that this was a tale that must be told.

In 1979 Allen's wife, Ruth, and I traveled to Liberia to visit the places where Mother had lived and worked. We trudged through the jungles, rode canoes on murky rivers, and were carried on the backs of oarsmen as they waded to the shore. Everywhere, we met people who had known and loved Mother. They were full of dramatic stories, told with great enthusiasm and vivid detail. I filled dozens of tapes of Mother's "children," most of whom spoke the colorful and colloquial English of Liberia.

At the end of our trip we celebrated her 100th birthday in Greenville. Hundreds of people marched and sang in the sweltering sun, as only Africans can. They carried banners; they dressed us in matching traditional "lappas" (wraparound skirts we had a hard time keeping on).

I had visited Mother Eliza in the nursing home in Tyler, Texas, just before our trip. She was preaching from her wheelchair in the sitting room of the simple home. Before I could visit her again upon my return from Liberia, Mother Eliza George had died in a hospital in Tyler at the age of 100.

In 1989 my husband and I returned to Liberia to visit villages in the interior where Mother always had longed to take the gospel. This time Gus was planning to establish Christian schools in villages that had no education system. We traveled to Nimba

County, the farthest north on the border of Ivory Coast. The atmosphere was eerie and tense, not the enthusiastic and warm welcome we had enjoyed before.

We learned later that the people of this village were plotting with a rebel army to move across the country and take over the government. Two weeks after our visit war broke out, destroying the infrastructure of Liberia, killing and maiming thousands, and causing thousands more to flee across the border. God had marvelously protected us from this hidden danger. Today the Liberia we saw is gone—but the spirit of Mother Eliza George and her love for Christ lives on in those who have survived.

My deepest gratitude is expressed to Cecelia Davis, Mother's adopted daughter, for helping so graciously in the initial research; to Gus and Otheliah Marwieh, Mother's spiritual children, for countless hours of interviews and helpful corrections; to the many friends in Liberia who made Mother's life come alive for me; to Elle Mae Rundle and others of the "Eliza Davis George Clubs" who shared her story; to my secretaries, Carolyn Garner and Marilyn Marinkovitch for their faithful help; to Ruth Finley who so cheerfully traveled with me to Liberia to help unearth the story. And for the many others whom I cannot name who helped me piece together the amazing life of Mother Eliza Davis George.

chapter one

MILES TO MONROVIA
(1930)

The surging surf pounded the Liberian coastline, tossing the rowboat like a piece of cork. The sea was often treacherous here. For centuries Kru tribesmen had bravely faced the ocean's fury in these timeproven vessels.

Hauling out the day's catch in their hand-sewn nets, two Kru fishermen prepared to beach the craft for the night. Here the jungle hugged the shore as closely as the ocean would permit, their village concealed where the surging tide and the steamy rain forest met. Darkness fell suddenly near the equator, and the tribesmen were eager to get home before night engulfed the trail.

The Kru chatted amicably over their catch when they spotted three figures moving along the shore—a rare sight along this desolate coast. As the strangers drew closer the men were startled to see a "civilized" woman accompanied by two boys. A safari helmet readily distinguished the woman from her tribal counterparts. Heavy boots protected her feet from the sun-baked sand, and she wore a dark print Western dress. In her right hand a long stick helped propel her forward.

Behind her trudged the barefoot teenagers, dressed only in tattered shorts, a canvas bag dangling from the shoulder of one of the boys. The receding tide washed over their scorched feet.

13

The men stopped to watch in amazement as the unlikely trio approached. Why were they so many miles from the nearest settlement? Such civilized people should be living with the Americo-Liberians—the freed American slaves who had colonized this land more than a hundred years earlier.

The woman, taller than the Kru, carried herself erect even in the soft surf and shifting sand. She wiped the perspiration from her face and neck. Despite her obvious fatigue, a ready smile lit up her warm face.

Because of their contacts with the towns along the coast, the Kru understood English. "Where you come from, Mama?" one of the fishermen asked. "You far from home out here."

"Son, we've been walking all day. We left Greenville before daybreak this morning. I'm Mother Eliza Davis George, and these are two of my boys, Robert and Tosnoh. We are on our way to Monrovia."

"Where you come from, Mama? You far from home out here."

"Monrovia! You gonna walk there?" the astonished fishermen asked. "It takes more than three days by rowboat. How you gonna walk that far?"

Mother Eliza rested on her walking stick and wiped her perspiring face and neck once again. "The Lord will help us, son. But tell me, how far is it to the next village? I think Robert and Tosnoh are getting too tired to walk much farther tonight."

"The next civilized settlement is across the Sanquin River," one of them answered, "but you can't cross tonight. The tide is too high. We can take you over tomorrow if you want to stay in our village tonight."

At the offer of traditional tribal hospitality, the boys' faces broke into a grin. They knew this meant a good meal of rice and fish cooked in palm butter, and a mat on the floor of one of the huts in the village. They had grown up in just such a village before they came to Mother's mission school, and they remembered how their own mothers had often cooked for strangers traveling through the jungle.

Without hesitation Mother Eliza accepted the offer. Since coming to Africa from Texas sixteen years earlier in 1914, she had spent many nights in an African hut, sharing the simple fare with these hospitable tribal people. A grass mat on a dirt floor would be luxury compared to the unprotected beach with its stinging sand.

For a moment she forgot the urgency pressing her forward on her 200-mile walk to Monrovia. It would take at least five more days like this one—days of 100-degree temperature under a relentless sun, days of burning feet and parched throat, days of pushing her fifty-one-year-old body to the limit of endurance. From her previous trips by dugout canoe along this same shore she knew there were dozens of rivers and streams gushing into the ocean between here and Monrovia. Each one would take courage and ingenuity to cross.

"Children, let's pray and thank God for bringing us this far."

But for tonight God had provided a friendly village, a meal, and a sheltered place to sleep. Before the startled Kru had a chance to lead the way to the village, she dropped to her knees, saying, "Children, let's pray and thank God for bringing us this far."

Mother and the boys slept well on the floor of the chief's hut, untroubled by the scurrying rats and voracious mosquitoes. When the morning dawned bright, clear, and hot, they felt rested and ready for the day ahead. One of the chief's wives gave Eliza some rice and cold cassava, a common tuberous plant associated with tapioca, to add to the meager stores in her canvas bag. Filling her jug from the drum of water the chief's daughters had hauled from the river, Mother prepared for the day's hike.

The fishermen led them back to the sea, ferrying them along the coast and across the wide Sanquin River, where they deposited the travelers on the eastern shore.

Mother Eliza thanked the fishermen profusely, reminding them once more of the Scripture she had taught them around the fire the night before. As the Kru pulled away from the shore she called out, "God bless you, my sons, for your kindness to Mother."

Though the air was already hot and sultry, the early hours of the morning were easier to bear. The sands had cooled during the night. An occasional whisper of a breeze off the ocean fanned the travelers.

Today Mother Eliza was more suitably dressed than when she had first arrived in Liberia. Her dress had short sleeves and an open neck, but her skirts were still long and full, and her rubber boots reached halfway up her calves. She would need them for this day's walk! She wore a pith helmet, which had become her trademark as she'd walked up and down the jungle trails these many years.

Robert and Tosnoh scampered ahead of her, pushing each other into the surf. They picked up unusual shells to bring back for Mother to see, while she pondered her life in Africa as she plodded over the sand.

chapter two

A TINY ENEMY

(1928)

*J*ust two years earlier, the Georges had returned to Liberia from a lengthy eight-year furlough in the United States. Though only eight miles inland from the seaport of Lexington, very little news made its way from the mission station of Kelton into the town. Their friends in the seaport could tell them nothing about the station.

Prior to the furlough, Mr. George and the boys had prepared hundreds of planks for building. The foundation of heavy cement blocks had been set and the framework constructed.

"With the supplies and tools we've brought with us, it shouldn't take more than a few weeks to finish our house," he assured Eliza. "We can stay in the old thatched hut until then, since most of the children haven't come back to school yet."

But the station held an unpleasant surprise.

As they neared the mission, it was a relief to emerge from the swamp and set their feet on a solid trail. Vines overhung the jungle path, and umbrella and cork trees provided dense shade.

Hurrying ahead, Mother waded across a brackish creek that seeped away into the underbrush. Coming to a fork in the trail, she instinctively turned toward the mission. Suddenly she saw a young African coming toward her. She put her hand over her eyes to shield them from the blinding sun.

"Why, son, son—can this be little Jimmy? I don't believe it—you've grown so tall." Turning, she called back along the trail, "Mr. George, come here. Look who's come to welcome us." And then in her typical fashion, she put her hand on Jimmy's shoulder, closed her eyes, and with her face turned into the brilliant African sunshine, she prayed:

Dear Lord, now thank you for bringing us here today. Thank you for keeping Jimmy safe these many long years we've been away. May we praise your name as we endeavor to serve you among these precious native people who need to know your love. Amen.

"Son, have you come to take us back to the mission with you?" she asked as Father George caught up with them and joined in the happy reunion. Jimmy's face, so radiant with happiness at seeing his beloved "parents," suddenly fell with apprehension. Years later he described the scene.

"I dropped my face. I frowned plenty 'cause the mission it broke down. I told Mother Eliza, 'The buga-bugs they eat everything!'"

"What do you mean, Jimmy?" Father George inquired sharply. "What about all the planks we sawed and piled up for the house? Surely you don't mean they've been destroyed."

Apprehensive, Father George now took the lead as the little troupe followed him across the last creek before the mission. A desolate sight met their eyes—the termites had indeed destroyed everything. The thatched hut that had been the Georges' first home had fallen in, its mat walls folded over, brown and dead. Time and the elements had claimed the leaves of the sagging thatched roof. Thick jungle growth strangled what remained.

Peering through the window in the one wall that still partially stood, Mother could see the remains of boxes of books and papers, soaked by rains and eaten by the busy termites.

It was hard to imagine that those tiny ants could do so much damage. But African termites are relentless in their quest for survival. The queen may live for twenty years in her dark, dank cell, producing up to 30,000 eggs a day. She and her multitudinous army had done their work well. Every paper, book, piece of furniture, plank, footing, and thatch had succumbed to their tireless mandibles. What the termites had not completely destroyed, the moisture and mold had claimed.

Father and Mother looked at each other in despair. Mr. George stalked off to check the lumber he had left stacked for building, Jimmy trailing behind him. The porters sat on their haunches where they had dropped their burdens, watching to see what this God-woman from across the sea would do.

"God has brought us here to do His work, and He'll help us through this."

Young Maude's chin quivered as she forlornly surveyed the place she once knew as home. The native Liberian girl, now sixteen, had accompanied Mother Eliza to America eight years ago. *What was Mother going to do now?* she wondered. Mother reached for the disappointed teenager: "Come here, Maudie—this isn't the end of the world. God has brought us here to do His work, and He'll help us through this."

Dropping to her knees and drawing Maude down beside her, Mother presented her petitions to her heavenly Father, confident that He would hear her.

Rising quickly, Mother resolved not to let the others see her discouragement. Summoning the porters, she called to her children: "We'll just have to go back to Lexington today, and tomorrow we'll see about buying more material to build the station. If we hurry, we can get through the swamp before dark."

chapter three

LIFE AT KELTON
(1928)

While Mr. George supervised the hiring of men and the purchasing of materials, Eliza began to re-gather the schoolchildren from the villages. Some had married and would not return to school, while others had lost interest and were content to stay home. But some of the parents, formerly resistant to any effort to educate their children, were now willing to let them go to the mission. Soon Mother would even have several little girls in her care, a new development in the Liberian bush.

As soon as Mr. George completed a two-room thatch hut, Mother and some of the children moved out to Kelton. Aware of the scarcity of food, Mother was eager to act. A garden was hastily planted, and she put even the youngest girls to work hoeing and weeding. Tools were scarce. Mother used a big hoe she brought from the States, but the girls had to use "pot hoes"—nothing more than thick sticks—to make rows for planting rice.

There was nothing Mother wouldn't do on the mission. She made herself a real Liberian.

Genevieve Mason, just ten years old when she moved to the mission from the bush, remembers Mother climbing onto the roof to help thatch one of the buildings. "There was nothing Mother wouldn't do on the mission," says Genevieve. "She made herself a real Liberian. She knew that she wasn't able to get her things from home. God even fixed it so that Mother Eliza could eat anything."

Being "a real Liberian" was the secret not only of Mother's acceptance by the people but of her very survival. Help from the churches in the United States was rare. The Georges hadn't expected to replace everything on the station when they returned, and the debts quickly mounted.

Praying for funds from America was part of the Georges' daily routine.

With so many children coming to the mission, Father George soon put up a separate house for the boys. Though constructed only of thatch siding and roofing, the buildings nevertheless required funds for lumber, framing, and labor. Mr. George was often harsh with the children, but without his strict supervision of the boys the work could never have been accomplished.

Praying for funds from America was part of the Georges' daily routine. When the mail arrived, there was always great expectancy. The mission agency sent money regularly, but Mother Eliza singled out two special gifts in her autobiography, *My Call to Africa*.

> "A letter was received from Mrs. Morris of Mineral Wells, Texas, enclosing a check for $100, half of which was donated by her. She said that she had heard Maude speak when she was in the United States and was interested in our work."

A second gift of eighty dollars came from her ever-faithful friend, Pastor S. A. Pleasant of St. John's Baptist Church in Houston, Texas. The accompanying note informed her that the church had decided to take up an offering for Kelton Mission every Tuesday evening.

Still, the financial pressures mounted. In their isolation, the Georges were unaware of the worldwide effects of the 1929 financial crash. Incoming funds were always insufficient to pay the debts, provide food and other necessities, and continue the building for the growing work.

It soon became apparent that one of them would have to go back to the American churches to share the need in Liberia. Still feeling the sting of the devastation when the mission was left uninhabited before, they dared not both leave. Reluctantly they decided that Mr. George would return to the USA while Mother remained to care for the children at Kelton.

Many a night Mother cried out to God in desperation.

After almost a year, Father George still had not been able to send much money. Meanwhile the situation at Kelton was deteriorating. The children knew that Mother fasted and prayed for funds to take care of the mission, but they could not sense the desperation that was beginning to grip her heart.

To make do, Mother bought supplies on credit from every store in Greenville, a nearby port town and trading center. The shopkeepers trusted her and appreciated the good work she was doing, but they could extend no more credit, and her cupboards were bare. Her supply of rice was almost gone, and the new crop would not be ready for months. The school needed staples— flour, sugar, and salt. Most of the children had only the clothes they wore on their backs. Few had blankets for the chilly nights of the approaching rainy season.

Many a night Mother cried out to God in desperation:

O heavenly Father, thou hast taught us to pray for our daily bread. Lord, thou dost know that I do not have one penny to buy food and pay the workers here at the mission. Father, send us something to meet our needs as thou hast promised. Help me to keep trusting thee so that the children will know thou art caring for them.

Though she encouraged the children to be thankful for their meager meals, it broke her heart to see their thin arms and legs. In desperation she sent them out to scratch for tasteless roots to add bulk to their monotonous diet.

It had now been months since gifts of any kind had reached the mission. The long tentacles of the Wall Street crash had touched the Liberian shores, and steamers rarely visited the port of Sinoe County. Not only the mission but the whole country was suffering.

In spite of their poverty, Mother determined that the children would not go naked. The younger ones would have been delighted to go without clothing in the tropical heat; yet she made sure that each child was at least minimally clothed. That meant constant patching and mending, even cutting up her own slips and dresses to make something for them.

But the financial crisis continued—until a ship at long last entered the Sinoe harbor. When Mother heard that the steamer had stopped at Greenville, she hastily made arrangements to go to town by "ankle express," as she called the long walk. Confident that there would be gifts for the mission in the mail, she took Robert and Tosnoh and several of the other younger children with her to help carry groceries. The rest of the children were excited to see them go. Mail usually meant extra food and parcels of clothing. It had been a long time since they had enjoyed that.

Arriving in Greenville late that afternoon, they went straight to the post office. There were a few letters from her family, which Mother pocketed to be read at her leisure back at the mission. Excited to see a letter from her husband, she opened it eagerly, hoping he had enclosed money for the mission. Her heart sank—nothing! Glancing through his letter, she learned that he had been very ill and had been unable to hold many meetings. But he assured her, "I'm fine now and have a busy schedule planned."

Then he added a cheering note, "A gift of several hundred dollars has been sent to you by one of the churches that learned of our need. I hope you have received it."

Eliza glanced frantically through the remaining letters, but there was nothing from a church or from the mission. One last letter from the post office in Monrovia remained. Tearing it open, she read:

> A postal order for $200 has been received for you.
> Return this form with your signature within 30 days.

But the letter was dated four weeks earlier!

Eliza stood in a little island of despair as the happy and boisterous crowds of Africans pushed past her. Staring at the stark missive in her hand, she couldn't believe what she had read.

Lord, how could this have happened? she thought. *Who could have made such a mistake as to send the money to Monrovia rather than here?* But when she looked at the children pressing around her, she remembered that her heavenly Father loved them more than she did.

"Sometimes when God answers prayer, He expects us to do our part too."

She drew her little brood closer and tried to explain. "Children, praise God, the money has come; but it isn't here in Greenville. You know, sometimes when God answers prayer, He expects us to do our part too. He has sent the money to Monrovia. Mother will just have to find a way to get it from there."

Robert was the first to comprehend her words. "But Mother, the steamship is gone, and there won't be one for months again." And then his lip began to tremble as he realized that, steamship or canoe, what did it matter? There was no money to go by any kind of vessel to Monrovia, two hundred miles up the coast.

Drawing on the persistent faith that had brought her to Africa against all odds, a plan took shape in Mother's mind. She knew that with just a little more effort on her part, the money was within reach. As she herded the little group down the road, she reassured them, "We'll just go and stay with Rev. Birch here in town tonight. God will show us what to do."

What God was showing her was plain and simple—the only way to get that money was to go to Monrovia. Since she had no money to hire a boat, she would just have to walk!

chapter four

ANKLE EXPRESS

$\mathcal{M}$other Eliza had never noticed that the sea was so noisy. Sailing across the ocean to Africa, she'd heard only the wind as it whistled past her on the deck and the steady swish-swish of the ship dipping into the rollers. In the evenings she had stood by the rail, straining her eyes into the darkness, hoping for a glimpse of the distant Liberian shore. The silver moonlight across the water was a peaceful beacon leading to her dream.

But here along the shore the ocean roared incessantly, beating against her ears like an African drum. She watched Robert and Tosnoh do what boys do on beaches—racing on ahead in search of pebbles and driftwood, marveling over a blue bottle washed up on shore, balancing themselves precariously on the huge black rocks God had sculpted on the beach. When the heat became unbearable they threw themselves into the surf, laughing and shouting as the waves toppled them like playful kittens. Mother knew there were dangerous undertows along the shore. She watched anxiously whenever they were in the water. "Be careful, children!" she shouted over the roar of the waves, though she knew they could not hear her.

By midday the heat became so unbearable that even the dignified Mother Eliza threw herself into the sea, clothes and all. The boys scrambled back to join her, and for a few minutes they forgot the heat and their blistered feet—and the urgency of their journey.

But most of the time Mother simply trudged along the shore, placing one foot in front of the other, one step closer to Monrovia, to the post office, to the money order waiting for her there.

Mother had felt at home here these sixteen years. Even this desolate, forbidding coastline was hers, and the tribal people to whom she had come to bring God's message of love were her brothers and sisters. As the overwhelming urgency of her journey to Monrovia gripped her, Eliza's indomitable faith surfaced. "Heavenly Father," she pleaded, "You brought me here to tell these children about you. You know they are hungry and that we have no money. Help me to reach Monrovia in time."

Tosnoh and Robert disappeared over the sandy ridge ahead. Mother had been lagging behind them all afternoon. Removing her heavy boots, she walked for a while in the cool ocean water. Salt stung the raw blisters that had popped up into fat bubbles on her heels, then burst like bubble gum and were now open and bleeding. But the coolness of the saltwater was preferable to the searing sand.

Eliza lost track of time. "Let's see, this must be Wednesday," she mused aloud, the constant roar of the surf drowning out her words. "No, it's Thursday. We left on Tuesday morning before the sun rose—yes, this is the third day. It's Thursday."

Then, as if to defy the relentless pounding of the sea, she began to sing a song she had composed the first day on the beach.

When your path is dark and your heart shrinks with fear,
When all seems lost and failure seems near,
Keep a clear, steady mind—just work, watch, and pray;
Jesus knows, loves, cares, and will your cause defray.
Just keep on, victory is ahead;
Look to Jesus, who multitudes fed.
He's the Son of God, the Living Bread;
He's the Ruler and the great Head.

27

A daring wave, getting ahead of the tide, slapped against Mother. As the undertow pulled the sand out from beneath her feet, she steadied herself and kept right on singing, louder than before.

Just keep on going on when your spirit's low,
When you've done your best and success seems slow,
By faith trust His word, keep His righteous command;
Fill your heart with song, whether on sea or land.
With five small fishes and two loaves of bread,
Large hungry crowds Jesus liberally fed.
If you give tithes of all you have in store,
He will shake, press down, and multiply more.

"That's true," Eliza thought. "Sometimes I have so little at Kelton to give the children—a few dried cassavas and some palm nuts they find in the jungle." She shook her head in wonder.

"They don't like palm nuts. I don't like palm nuts either, but at least it's something to eat when there's no money. And so far we haven't starved. It's like the loaves and the fishes—they weren't much, but nobody starved."

> "It's like the loaves and the fishes—they weren't much, but nobody starved."

Eliza stumbled and caught herself with her walking stick to keep herself from sprawling headlong into the sand. "Where are those boys? They'd better come and help me. I must—keep—going. Mama always said, 'Don't quit. If you've got a job to do, don't quit.' Oh, Mama, what would you say if you knew I was walking two hundred miles in Africa to get $200?" Then she chuckled to herself, "You always told me I'd do something special."

chapter five

AFTER SLAVERY
(1839–1900)

Thoughts of Mama brought a torrent of memories to Eliza's mind. Her mother had died just before this trip to Africa. Her greatest source of encouragement and prayer support was suddenly gone.

Jane Burdick was born a slave on the Burdick plantation in Bastrop County, Texas, in 1839. She had often told Eliza what it felt like to stand on the block to be sold.

"Liza, I was so scared. But God meant it to me for good, cause the Woodmores were so nice. And that's where I met your papa."

Eliza could never hear the story enough—how Mama had been sitting on the fence smoking her pipe when Papa came along. Doffing his faded blue work cap, Litt Davis greeted her formally, "How do you do, Lady?"

Jane, his elder by two years, haughtily replied, "How do you do, son?" But she couldn't resist his unabashed admiration and good humor that made him one of the most popular young blades in the quarters. After a suitable courtship period, they "jumped the broom" and became man and wife. Eight years later the Emancipation Proclamation gave them their freedom.

Jane was a praying woman who spoke often of her "brothers and sisters" in Africa. When she was young she dreamed of going to the continent of their forefathers. Eliza wrote in her autobiography, *My Call to Africa*, "I have always felt that her desire was transmitted to me—the desire to see Africa."

Eliza was the third of Litt and Jane Davis's eleven children. Her mother's prayers were part of Eliza's earliest memories. At the end of the long days in the cotton fields, Jane would drop to her knees beside the patchwork-covered bed and pray in a moaning melodic tone, her voice rising and falling with the rhythm of the words.

O heavenly Father,
This evening, Father, is the end of another long day.
O I thank you for keeping me through the day,
And now here I am on my knees giving you praise.
Bless the offspring of my dying body;
Help me to raise them up in the way you'd have them go.

One day as Jane was working in the garden she heard Eliza's voice from behind the hedges at the end of the yard. Stepping closer, she heard the lilting young voice, "O Lord, bless the off-spring of my dying body."

"Liza, whatever are you doing?" Jane broke in. "Offspring is children—you ain't got no children!"

Large families were an advantage for the sharecroppers. Litt Davis worked one hundred acres of cotton, and Eliza and her two older brothers helped pick cotton when they were barely old enough to see over the tops of the popping bushes. Sometimes she stayed home to take care of sister Mary and baby Willy while Mama worked under the hot sun.

Even with the best of crops and the biggest of families, Litt struggled financially. Since he furnished his own food, imple-ments, and horses, he received two-thirds of the profits from the sales. But a huge bill awaited him at the end of every summer, and he never had quite enough to pay it off.

One temptation for making extra money was gambling. Night after night Litt and the other men from the quarters played cards, hoping to win from each other what they had lost the night before.

Litt had a winning streak one night that sent him home walking on air. Oh, how Jane would thank him now! With a flourish,
he would toss the $100 into her lap. "All yours, Janie," he would
say proudly. "We can pay our debt to Mr. Woodmore, you can
buy yourself a new dress, and there's enough for shoes for all the
children."

But it didn't happen quite that way. Jane was mending socks,
sitting near the lamp to benefit from its soft light. When he
dropped the bills onto her ample lap, she looked up in disgust.

"Litt Davis, I don't need the Devil's money," she said, fling-
ing the cash through the open window. Speechless, Litt backed
off, unable to comprehend her rejection of his gift. He sneaked
away into the darkness and didn't return until morning.

But things were to change. One day when Eliza was seven
years old, "Miss Ann," wife of the plantation owner, asked Litt to
drive the buggy to a nearby town. She wanted to hear the famous
singing evangelist, Ira Sankey.

Arriving at the meeting house, Litt parked the buggy near
the side of the building, where he would be shaded from the sun
while he waited for Miss Ann. Those were the days when black
people didn't enter white folks' houses!

But on this hot afternoon all the windows of the church were
open, and Sankey's voice easily carried out across the sleepy
churchyard. Try as he might, Litt could not sleep. Flies buzzed
incessantly around the horse and its sweaty driver. He couldn't
help overhearing Sankey's message: "The wages of sin is death,
but the gift of God is eternal life." The piercing voice of the
evangelist rose higher as Sankey warmed up to his subject. "I dare
say some of you fathers here are gambling men. Your wife is
probably praying for you right now."

Litt grew angry under the sound of that penetrating message. *Surely it was directed right at me*, he told himself. *Miss Ann*

brought me here for a purpose. Jane must have been telling her about my gambling.

On the ride home, he replied to Mrs. Woodmore's enthusiastic report of "dear Brother Sankey's message" with monosyllabic grunts. He wasn't going to let on he'd heard a thing!

The next night Jane attended her usual weekly meeting at the nearby Baptist church. Litt had been going with her, more or less to keep the peace. But he began to suspect a conspiracy when Rev. Walker spoke on the very same text, warning the drunkards and gamblers in the audience of their doom.

Litt was furious! Heads turned as he grumbled to Jane, "I'm not standing for this. You told that preacher about me, and I'm not listening to any more!"

Horrified, Jane saw him get up to leave the meeting. Everyone in the congregation turned to watch.

Eliza could tell the story as though she'd seen it all herself. "Papa just fell down hollering, and he couldn't help himself. 'Lord, have mercy!' he cried. He said if the Lord would let him get up, he would never do such a thing again.

"He got up and stumbled out of the church into the graveyard. He fell down again, and stayed there all night next to the grave of a man he used to gamble with. When Papa got up, he got up born-again Litt."

From that time until his death in 1947, Litt Davis was a faithful deacon of the Baptist church, and a powerful preacher too.

Litt's conversion was so dramatic that many others in the small black community also repented. Eliza loved to tell of Mr. Tippler Henry, who often gambled with her father. While sitting around the card table, someone informed him of Litt's repentance. Tippler jumped up crying, "You telling me that Litt is converted?" And Eliza added triumphantly, "Tippler was converted right there on the spot!"

Litt was not an educated man. Slavery had succeeded in keeping most black men out of school. But he had learned to read a little, and he could quote the Bible at length.

Jane longed for her children to be educated, and she inspired Eliza to aim at becoming a teacher. "Liza, you're going to do something special one day," she would say. In later years Eliza taught her own mother how to read and write.

Whenever the children could be spared from the farm work, the Davises encouraged them to go to school, a dilapidated little schoolhouse that opened for only a few months in the winter. The children grandly referred to their teacher as "Professor Lawyer Taylor."

Eliza was not accomplished in math. But "Papa would help us," she recalled. "He would say, 'Liza, if a bale of cotton weighs 655 pounds and is selling at 11 1/2 cents a pound, how much would it cost?' While we were getting out our pencils, Papa figured it all out."

Eliza's heart had been softened by the gospel her parents lived.

It was soon evident that Eliza Davis was somebody who was going places. Her leadership ability didn't always take her in the right direction, however. Reports came back to Teacher Taylor that some of the children had been stealing plums on the way home from school. The next morning Eliza arrived in the classroom to see blazoned across the blackboard these accusing words: "Plum thieves, Eliza Davis, chairman."

But Eliza's heart had been softened by the gospel her parents lived. And she loved to attend the lively worship services at the Baptist church.

There weren't many copies of the "old 800" hymnal in the church, so most people learned the hymns by memory. When they sang, they sang from their hearts, their bodies swaying and hands clapping with joy.

Go preach my gospel, saith the Lord;
Let this whole earth my grace receive. . . .
He shall be saved who trusts the Lord,
And he condemned who will not believe.

Sometimes Eliza sat on the hill overlooking the river, watching the baptismal services below. She wanted to go down and be baptized, but she didn't yet fully understand why.

When she was sixteen the pastor of the Baptist church, Elder Martin Hurd, approached her. "Eliza, you've been coming to church every Sunday, hearing the preaching of the Word of God. Don't you think you could trust the Lord as your personal Savior?"

Eliza's clear brown eyes looked right back into his. "Yes, Brother Hurd, if I believe on Him, I know He'll save me."

But it wasn't until the next series of revival meetings that Eliza moved forward to the "mourners' bench," where those under conviction would stay until they made their decision. Eliza recalled, "I went to the mourners' bench the first night and began to tremble. I stayed on it for about five nights during the special meetings.

"Then Mr. Hurd delivered a sermon on John 3:16, one I shall never forget. It answered my heart, and I accepted the Lord—and never felt so happy in my life. Immediately there seemed to be in my thoughts a longing to do something for Him, but what that something was I did not know."

> "Immediately there seemed to be in my thoughts a longing to do something for Him, but what that something was I did not know."

That "something" set Eliza apart when it came to the young men, who were more and more the center of her girlfriends' conversations. Giggling and whispering, the girls told about furtive love notes and "accidental" meetings on the way to school.

Eliza held herself aloof, and the boys soon caught on. When a new boy was introduced to the Davis girls after church on a Sunday morning, the conversation usually went something like this: "Mr. Henry Jones, this is Miss Mary Davis, and this is her sister, Miss Eliza Davis. She is a *senior.*" Eliza's cool "how-do-you-do" implied, "Don't get too close. I have something *special* to do."

But Eliza met her match in Phil, who twisted her heart around his finger with his suave words and worldly-wise ways. Walking home from church through the freshly mown fields, grasshoppers jumping up as they kicked the little piles of hay aside, Phil asked, "Will you go to the ice cream social with me on Saturday night? There's nobody else I'd like to take as much as you, Miss Davis!"

It took all her control for Eliza to say, "Thank you, Mr. Phil, but I will have to ask my parents." As soon as Phil turned off the lane toward his farm, Eliza flew home, her long legs skimming over the grounds as they did in the days when she was chosen the best ballplayer in the school.

Kneading bread dough in the hot, sun-filled kitchen, Mama listened to Eliza's request in silence. Then she said thoughtfully, "Child, you can go if Papa agrees. But, Eliza, if you're goin' to go to college, go to college. Don't have no truck with a boy like Phil."

Hardly daunted, Eliza changed her school clothes and saddled her mother's horse, Seelom. The horse seemed to sense her jubilation and needed little urging to cover the miles to her friend Mary's home so she could tell her the exciting news.

But Mary was bursting with her own news. As soon as the girls could slip away to their favorite hideaway in the orchard, Mary burst out, "Oh Eliza, I'm so happy. Phil was here last night, and he told me that he loves me!"

A heartbroken Eliza rode back home, suffering her first pain of unrequited love, too willful to accept her defeat. Stopping to mull over the situation, she heard the mournful call of a dove perched in the lower branches of a tree along the road. "He sounds like I feel," complained Eliza. Then she closed her eyes and in her strong young voice spoke out, "Lord, if it's your will that I marry Phil, I want that dove to fly from that tree when I open my eyes."

She laughingly recalled, "That dove wouldn't fly. I got so mad I picked up a rock and threw it at it."

The next afternoon Eliza was plowing some land that Mama wanted dug up for planting turnips. Eliza was glad to get out of the house to plod slowly through the moist-smelling sod behind Paul, one of her father's mules. It gave her time to think. But the more she thought about Phil, the angrier she became. Suddenly she burst out loud, "How could Phil do this to me?" only to see her mother coming across the field toward her. Not wanting her mother to know how upset she was, she began singing. Mama never did catch on!

Later that evening Papa came to Eliza saying that Mama had told him about Phil. "I didn't want to tell you this, Honey, but Phil has already been married. He married a very nice girl, Mr. Mouton's daughter. She has two children. And he quit her, just like that. Carol is one of the sweetest girls you'd want to meet. And if he gets you, he'll quit you too."

Eliza squeezed Papa's arm. She didn't tell him he'd already done just that.

Other proposals, more serious in intent, would come. But every time a suitor made his declaration, Eliza would quickly make hers. There was "something special" that God wanted her to do.

chapter six

THE CALL TO AFRICA

(1900–1913)

*N*ineteen-hundred was a dark year for the Davis family.
First, the boll weevils destroyed their entire cotton crop.
Papa went off to look for a job, and the family didn't hear from
him for weeks. Paul, Betty, Luke, and Bill—their four faithful
mules—had to be mortgaged. Then their horse Seelom was sold.

At age twenty, Eliza had spent one year at Guadalupe College, a teachers' training college forty miles from home. She
loved it—everything but math! Eliza had hoped that her earnings
for picking cotton would pay her school fees for the next year.
At fifty cents per hundred pounds, she could save a substantial
portion of the thirty-eight dollars she needed for the year.

But now the crop was gone, and Papa was gone. It seemed all
hope of returning to Guadalupe College was gone too.

For a black girl in the South at the turn of the twentieth century, attending a teachers' training college was remarkable. With
slavery dead for only thirty-five years, few black children aspired
even to a high-school education. Southern whites scoffed at
Negroes who got an education instead of continuing to labor in
the fields.

But Eliza worked hard, and her family sacrificed to pay the
fees. The Bible classes and devotional sessions at the school were
helping her mature, and she was beginning to understand what
God might want her to do. During a chapel service Rev. H. Bouey,

fresh from a trip to Liberia, challenged the student body to missionary service. Eliza was one of the three students who responded to his invitation, and the seed of a plan was sown in her breast.

But 1900 dashed those hopes.

One morning toward the end of that devastating summer, Eliza borrowed a horse to ride to town to get a few necessities for the family. Hoping for a letter from Papa, she stopped to ask for mail at the post office.

To her surprise the postmistress handed her a letter from Guadalupe College. Tearing it open, she could hardly believe her eyes as she read: "Dear Miss Eliza, 'Trust in the Lord and do good; so shalt thou dwell in the land. In all thy ways acknowledge Him, and He shall direct thy paths.' We heard that the boll weevils destroyed your parents' cotton crop, so special arrangements have been made for you to enter college this year. Come at once!"

When Eliza returned to Guadalupe she found that the "special arrangements" included a part-time job in the school kitchen. Every evening she mixed dough for the next day's bread in a huge tub and let it set in the warm kitchen overnight. At 4:30 the next morning she was up baking.

Between the little she earned in the kitchen and the egg money that Mama sent, she managed. She recalled, "Mama used to send me ten cents in an envelope. We used to get ten cents a dozen for eggs. I would get change and take out one cent for a tithe."

Then in the spring of 1901 Eliza received a phone call from her brother-in-law in Bastrop. As she flew down the hall to take the call in the president's office, her mind conjured up a thousand cries. "Is it Papa? Has he been hurt? Or is Mama sick?"

Grabbing the phone, Eliza heard, "You've got to come home. Willy took a fit and fell into the fire. The doctor says he's dyin'."

Standing at the bedside of her dying brother, Eliza could see that her mother had reached the breaking point. Her father was still not home, though word had come that he was trying to find a place for the family to live in Tyler, Texas. Slipping quietly out of the sickroom, Eliza went to the well-used, carved oak pump organ that was the family's prize possession, and began playing vigorously. "Ask the Savior to help you; He will comfort and bless you, He will carry you through."

Willy died. At the funeral in Antioch, Uncle Ike, a licensed preacher, asked Eliza to say a few words.

"I was at school when the message came. I got home to find Mama

> "Papa has mortgaged everything we have—we ain't got nothin' at all now."

tryin' to keep a big heart. Papa has mortgaged everything we have—we ain't got nothin' at all now. Looks like everything has gone against us, but Jesus has promised never to leave us alone."

Watching Mama in the front row, Eliza saw her sagging shoulders straighten with resolve. "Mama got happy and never did cry," she says.

On the way home from the funeral, Eliza broached the subject of going back to school.

"Mama, I've decided to stay home and help you. When Papa gets a job and things are better, I can go back again. But for now, you need me at home."

Her mother wouldn't hear of it. "No, no, Eliza, you must go back. When I'm dead and buried and my bones are bleached in the earth, you'll have need of this training. God will carry us through this trouble too."

Eliza completed her second year at Guadalupe, earning a teacher's diploma. Since there were so few black teachers, teachers' training colleges used senior students to teach younger children while completing their own courses. Eliza got a job in Waco, Texas, teaching the younger grades, while she worked toward her teacher's certificate at Central Texas College. Things had improved at home too. Her father found employment and purchased a house for the family in Tyler.

After completing her academic course at Central Texas College, Eliza joined the faculty. She taught for five years before the school asked her to serve as matron.

On February 2, 1911, the faculty and students gathered for their usual morning devotional hour. As the students filed in they saw that Professor Hill would be leading the devotion. Eliza overheard one of the boys say to his friend, "Here we go, all the way around the world and halfway back again."

While Rev. Hill prayed for India, China, Japan, and Africa, Eliza's heart was suddenly filled with an overwhelming desire to see her brothers and sisters in Africa. It seemed as though her soul swelled and grew so that her body was a tiny core of her real self. As clearly as if she were there, she saw Africans passing before the judgment seat of Christ, weeping and moaning, "But no one ever told us You died for us."

> Eliza's heart was suddenly filled with an overwhelming desire to see her brothers and sisters in Africa

Eliza sat in her seat long after the students had fled the chapel, released from their unwilling captivity. When she finally got up to return to her office she met the school president, Dr. John Strong, who noticed her unusually pensive behavior.

Touching her elbow, he asked with concern, "Are you all right, Miss Davis?"

Eliza blurted out, "I'm fine, Dr. Strong. I'm going to Africa."

"Oh, please, Miss Davis, don't let yourself get carried away by that foolishness," he remonstrated. "You don't have to go over there to be a missionary—we have enough Africa over here!"

Two years later Eliza sat at her desk, her back straight and unbending, even after ten hours a day on her feet. A matron's job included many things—cleaning the toilets, checking dirty linens, ordering groceries. It seemed she ran all day long, with never a minute to catch her breath.

But this letter had to be written—and written carefully.

She started again, "Dear Dr. Strong and members of the Board of Trustees of Central Texas College. . . ."

She had composed the letter so often in her mind as she rushed from one task to another during the day that it ought to have come easily. But resignations are seldom easy to write— especially this one. Eliza knew that the faculty thought her idea of going to Africa was crazy. More than one teacher had told her so.

It was now two years since God had spoken to her so clearly in that morning chapel. Though she had most emphatically told Dr. Strong her plans, a trip to Africa had been out of the question at the time. There were still six brothers and sisters at home. (Mary had died just a few years after Willy.) Eliza had been helping Jenny Belle, Ellen, and Vic through school.

But now there were others in the family who could help Papa, and the time had come when she could begin to fulfill her own God-given ambition. She began again:

Dear Dr. Strong:
It is with deep regret that I find it necessary to tender my resignation as matron of Central Texas College. God has called me to serve my brethren in Africa, and I can no longer refuse. Please accept my resignation as of the end of the school year.

Sincerely, Eliza L. Davis

What had seemed a simple matter turned into a furor. The board members certainly did not agree that Miss Davis should go to Africa as a missionary. They reminded her that the Negro in

America was far worse off than his African brothers were. The battle for equality and education had just begun. They needed her at the college—she was the best fundraiser they had.

Though sweetly refuting their arguments, Eliza found herself seething inside. "They just want me to keep cleaning the toilets and picking up after everyone because no one else wants to do it."

But a black woman had never gone out as a missionary from Texas before. The leaders of the Baptist Convention did not believe she was able to take on such a pioneering work.

A black woman had never gone out as a missionary from Texas before.

The president of the state convention came to speak with Eliza personally about her request. When he saw her stubborn determination, he told her he thought she was losing her mind.

"Miss Davis," he reprimanded sternly, "you don't have the money, and we ministers stand between you and the people to keep you from getting the money!"

Eliza did not answer him. But deep down her heart responded, "But you don't stand between me and my God!"

After weeks of arguments and discussions, the board agreed to call a special meeting at which Eliza could personally present her reasons for her decision. She spent sleepless nights working out her speech, painstakingly writing and rewriting, until she had it perfect.

At the same time, in her devotions God gave her a poem that expressed her longing. Its message unfolded like a flower, gripping her own heart and reinforcing her conviction that she was making the right decision. Whether the board agreed or not, she was determined to leave Central Texas College and prepare for the mission field. Somehow, somewhere, God would provide what she needed to go to Africa.

Eliza dressed carefully for the board meeting. Her white blouse was starched immaculately, the dozen pearl buttons sparkling. She tied her blue paisley tie as carefully as any man's, and her high-button shoes glistened.

Confidently she stood to present her case to the board. She read defiance in the eyes of some of the men, and a faintly bemused curiosity in others. Breathing a prayer for help, Eliza began.

"But you don't stand between me and my God!"

"Gentlemen, led by the Spirit of God, I have found my life's work. I believe God would have me go to Africa to take the gospel of salvation to the people in darkness."

As Eliza outlined her reasons for going, the defiant demeanors began to soften. The men listened intently to every word.

"Not only is the Holy Spirit calling me, but these are my brothers and sisters—your brothers and sisters. While we Negroes were brought here to America seemingly for our harm, God has used it for good. We have come to know Jesus Christ and are no longer bound in chains of witchcraft and heathenism. Just as Moses returned to his own people after he had learned the wisdom of the Egyptians, so I believe God wants me to go back and share with my lost brethren the education He has privileged me to get in America.

"I believe my life's work is not in America but Africa, and that's where I *must* go.

"In closing, I would like to recite a poem which God has led me to write in these past weeks as I've been struggling with my decision."

My African brother is calling me;
Hark! Hark! I hear his voice.
In a land more dense with work I see
That work is now my choice.

43

Glancing straight into the eyes of her most vocal antagonist, Eliza continued:

Would you say 'stay' when God said 'go'
To that dark foreign land and
Spread the light? Would you say 'no'
That bright their souls might stand?
There he bows down to wood and stone—
He thinks his way is right.
And when from earth his soul has gone,
To hell he takes his flight.

As Eliza's clear strong voice rang out, the men shifted uneasily in their chairs.

Christ on His throne could've been at ease
When all the world was lost,
But gave His life for death to please;
His lifeblood paid the cost.

My African brother awaits my call;
The Lord bids me now depart.
His word is firm and cannot fail;
I'll trust His Word and start.

Kindred and friends, I bid farewell—
I'm going on yonder shore.
The Word of God is mine to tell;
My brother is my store.

I'll work for him with all my might,
And try his heart to reach.
I'll work till age shall dim my sight;
I'll to him God's Word teach.

I'll look to God to guide my way
And trust His promise sure;
And since He leads I will not stray—
His Word is so secure.

And when on earth my time shall come
To stand before the King,
I'll see in Christ I did win some,
I'll hear my brothers sing.

Eliza sat down, realizing that she had never once even looked at the notes clenched in her hand. Then, startled, she heard the board members applauding. Dr. Strong stood up, looked at Eliza, and said:

"Miss Davis, your eloquence and sincerity have moved us deeply. I for one can no longer stand in the way of your fulfilling your life's ambition.

"I can sense that the rest of the members of the board feel as I do. We are not able to provide the necessary funds for your venture—you will have to trust God for that. But we can release you from further obligations to Central Texas College and assure you of our prayers."

Before Eliza finished the school year at Central, she met the man who was to be her friend and helper: Rev. James Kelly, the corresponding secretary of the Foreign Missions Board of the General Baptist Convention of Texas. As a part of the National Baptist Convention, the Texas group was responsible for any missionaries going out from Texas, and so Eliza came to Rev. Kelly's attention.

Rev. Kelly took Eliza to black churches in Houston, New Orleans, and elsewhere to help raise support. One church gave her a Singer sewing machine.

Word finally came from Dr. Jordan of the National Baptist Convention that she would be working with Miss Susie Taylor in

Fortesville, Liberia. A ship would be leaving from New York for Liverpool on December 12, 1913. Dr. Jordan would accompany her to New York.

Eliza never spoke of the farewells with her family in Texas. But one can imagine the mingled pride, joy, and sorrow as she kissed Mama and Papa goodbye, hugged her sisters and brothers, and tried not to look at Mama's tears and Papa's anguish as they stood in the doorway of the little clapboard house, watching her ride away. Liberia was a never-never land they could barely find on a map. It would be seven years before they saw Eliza again.

In New York, Eliza and Dr. Jordan stayed in the home of another missionary to Liberia. The following morning Dr. Jordan took Eliza to the docks and made sure that she was comfortably settled in her tiny cabin on the *Celtic*.

Standing at the rail as Dr. Jordan prepared to disembark, a terrifying thought struck Eliza. Putting her hand on his arm, she asked, "Dr. Jordan, how must I begin my work when I get to Africa?"

"Any way you can, my dear," he replied as he turned and walked down the gangplank.

chapter seven

THE LOVE OF LIBERTY

A sudden wave jolted Mother Eliza from her reverie. She had been so immersed in her thoughts that she hadn't noticed the sky turning black and the sea churning into a sullen gray cauldron. Far up the beach the boys were scurrying for cover under the overhang of a huge boulder. It was too late for Eliza to join them before the deluge fell.

Equatorial rainfalls, as nowhere else on earth, pour as if all the faucets of heaven had been opened at once. In seconds Eliza was soaked to the skin, shivering in the rapidly chilling air. Doggedly she kept going along the beach, one foot ahead of the other, one step closer to Monrovia.

By the following day the trio moved at a snail's pace across the hot sand. Robert and Tosnoh's feet, despite being toughened from a lifetime of going barefoot, were burned and blistered. Walking in the surf relieved the heat, but the saltwater stung their raw blisters.

Tosnoh took to walking on the sides of his feet. Mother Eliza couldn't help teasing him, "You look like a bowlegged cowboy from Texas."

No longer did the boys scamper ahead to play in the sand and surf. Mother had to urge them to keep up. "This is Friday, children; we should be there tomorrow night, or the latest on Sunday. But we must keep going so we can catch the steamer back to Greenville on Monday morning."

The thought of the steamer put new life into the boys for a few minutes, but soon they were complaining about their feet and how tired they were.

All her life Mother had amused and captured the hearts of children with her gift of storytelling. Putting her own aches and discomforts aside, she tried to take the boys' minds off their troubles.

But even Eliza's flair for the dramatic failed to hold the suffering boys' interest. Once more they lagged behind. And once again, Mother was alone with her memories.

> All her life Mother had amused and captured the hearts of children with her gift of storytelling.

Mother reflected back to the first time she had seen the burning sands of Liberia's coastline—and she recalled her undignified arrival on it!

"Come on, Mammy!" She could still hear the almost-naked black boy as he reached his hands up to steady Eliza as she looked down the rope ladder hanging from the *Celtic's* sides into the rough, handhewn canoe below.

The *Celtic* had arrived at Monrovia the morning of January 20, 1914, and had lain three miles out to sea, rocking in the gentle swells and the feverish sun. Eliza's long-sleeved cotton blouse, with the navy bow-tie tucked under her chin and the heavy worsted skirt, had captured the heat. Her cotton undershirt stuck to her body like her grandmother's mustard plasters. Once the ship struck anchor, the sea breeze, which had provided a modicum of relief from the heat, stopped completely.

Monrovia in 1914 was little more than a small town, with fewer than five thousand inhabitants. It had been settled by American slaves who had been freed in the early part of the nineteenth century and had tried to carve out a living in the hostile heat and humidity of Liberia. The twin perils of malaria and dysentery took the lives of over half the settlers in those early years.

The only street in Monrovia was nothing more than a winding path overrun with grass and obstructed by rocky outcroppings. Goats, cattle, and sheep grazed among the houses and outbuildings. Many of the buildings along the street were only half-completed, their owners' ambitious dreams outstripping reality. Grassy patches along the road served as the community laundry, where washing was spread to dry. Most of the buildings, whether occupied or incomplete, had a crumbling weather-beaten look. Anything made of wood or grass survived only a few seasons, as Eliza and Mr. George later learned.

Mother's first contact with the tribal people had given her a clear picture of what God wanted them to do in Liberia. Together with Susie Taylor they would reach the natives in the interior villages. First, however, they had to convince the Liberian Baptist Convention, with whom the National Baptists cooperated.

Mission work among tribal people was rare in those days. It was a dangerous venture to establish a work in the uncharted interior. It was doubly dangerous for women.

> It was a dangerous venture to establish a work in the uncharted interior.

Eliza had been shocked to learn that Liberia was divided into two distinct and separate population groups—the Americo-Liberians and the tribal people. Her first days in Monrovia quickly revealed that the descendants of the first colonists maintained a veneer of sophistication—a pride of heritage that confined their social contacts and political efforts.

Liberia's history is a rich and fascinating one, its roots growing out of antebellum America. In the early nineteenth century certain American whites grew restless over the slave situation and formed the American Colonization Society to find a place in

Africa where freed slaves could return to establish their own country.

Others who backed the project had less pure motives—many slave owners felt that the presence of large numbers of freed slaves would disturb the contentment of their own slaves.

The first contingent of freed slaves left the USA in the spring of 1820 and settled on Cape Montserrado, the site of present-day Monrovia. Of the eighty-six original settlers, forty-nine died within six months. The region was a hellhole of disease, with malaria, yellow fever, and dysentery running rampant. The colony had no doctor.

Settlers negotiated with tribal chiefs to purchase an area along the coast one hundred forty miles long and forty miles wide. The payment for the settlement of thirty huts included muskets, powder, basins, knives, walking sticks, hats, and shoes. The total cost for the goods was less than seventy-five dollars.

The tribal people were suspicious of the colonists.

But the tribal people were suspicious of the colonists. The region had been decimated by two centuries of slaving. Believing that the new arrivals were simply a ruse sent by slave traders, the tribalists prepared to attack.

Though more than 4,000 settlers had arrived by now, nearly 2,100 had succumbed to disease. Jehudi Ashmun, the second supervisor of the colony and one of a handful of white leaders, began training the survivors to defend themselves from the hostile tribes. When the attack came, women fought alongside men against natives armed with spears and battle-axes. A lone cannon gave the beleaguered colonists an advantage.

Ashmun did much to establish the colony. To enlist their cooperation, he denied all "drones" the privilege of drawing rations from the central storehouse.

It was difficult for the liberated slaves, who had known the horrors and degradation of slavery, to become productive workers for their new nation. Rather, they assumed the genteel attitudes they had observed in their own Southern masters, and preserved the traditions they brought with them from America. A social gathering became an occasion for formal dark suits, top hats, and long satin gowns. Their houses were an attempt at replicating Southern architecture, though with few materials and limited skills many of the structures were never completed.

The Colonization Society provided no funds for development. Yet they continued to dump untrained and impoverished settlers on Liberia's shores. There was a pathos about the stunted settlement with its follies built on the rocky hillside. The new Liberians were a people planted without money or home on a coast of yellow fever and malaria, left to make what they could of an Africa they did not know.

Yet motivated by their motto, "The love of liberty brought us here," the proud settlers struggled to carve a new country out of the hostile environment. The republic born in 1847 was the first independent nation in Africa.

The colonists soon became masters of diplomacy. Beginning with their first president, Joseph Jenkins Roberts, Liberia was ruled by a succession of able statesmen and stable governments until 1980, when President William Tolbert was assassinated in a coup d'etat.

As the fledgling nation took root, tribal people were drawn to the jobs and goods available in Monrovia. In the process, they became the unwitting servants of their colonial masters. Western clothing, the use of English, and Southern architecture—all the trappings of civilization, grew to be synonymous with the Americo-Liberian way of life. Christianity became equated with civilization as well, and the settlers gave the unfortunate impression that speaking English was a prerequisite to becoming a Christian.

In the early twentieth century the gravest problem facing Liberia continued to be the relationship of the Americo-Liberians and the sixteen major tribes, who comprised ninety percent of the population. The 1847 constitution, based on the American document, granted citizenship only to blacks, but limited the vote to those who owned property.

Liberia's founding fathers had come with a noble twin purpose—to snuff out slavery at its source and to bring Christianity to Africa. The first settlers formed a church onboard ship, and the Providence Baptist Church in Monrovia is the oldest permanent building in the country and the oldest Baptist church on the continent.

The settlers were faithful churchgoers, and many of the nation's early leaders were earnest Christians. But all too soon Christianity became a facade for civilization. Others used the church for their own social ends, living lives of immorality outside the church walls. Liberian church historian Conrad Wold sums up the era: "The strategy of early missionaries was to use the colonists as stepping stones to evangelization of tribes. But they never got past the stepping stones."

chapter eight

"SHE GOIN' TO KILL ME"
(1913–1916)

*W*hen Eliza first arrived in Liberia, she discovered well-attended Baptist and Methodist churches in all the civilized towns. Missionaries and pastors had been discouraged from taking the civilizing influence of Christianity to the tribes, but attitudes were beginning to change. Determined to get beyond the "stepping stones," Eliza and Susie overcame initial resistance and were granted permission to open a school for tribal children several miles into the interior.

For months Eliza and Susie prepared for the new mission. They decided to call it the Bible Industrial Academy, signifying the dual aim of the school—teaching the children to read the Bible, and showing them how to farm and do basic tasks that would make them productive citizens.

Mr. Reeves, a congressman who represented Fortesville in Monrovia, helped purchase the lumber and hire Liberian nationals to build a house on the site. But first, every inch of ground had to be cleared of centuries of heavy growth.

Eliza and Susie supervised the men as they cut saplings and built a mud house on a bamboo frame, covering it with palm thatch. The dirt floor was pounded, smoothed, and covered with mats. The two windows needed no glass, but Eliza showed the workers how to make wooden shutters that could be closed when the torrential rains beat against the house. To Eliza the two-room hut was beautiful. Until another one could be constructed, the little boys would be staying with them.

A happy procession of children headed out of Fortesville to the new mission school when it opened. On his head each one carried a box or basin; some children were almost hidden beneath their loads. They argued among themselves for the privilege of carrying the shiny new washtub, a gift from one of the women in the church.

In the months that followed, the women had more land cleared for farming. Susie had never made a Liberian farm before, so the tribal workers helped them, slashing the undergrowth with fierce-looking cutlasses and burning the brush to clear several acres of land at a time. How Eliza would have loved to have the faithful plodding mules from Papa's farm! Dutifully, she hoed the fertile soil, working long hours with the boys to plant cassava and roots, such as edoes, and even coffee scions.

Eliza traveled up and down the rivers and creeks by canoe.

During their first year at BIA, Susie and Eliza divided the responsibilities. Susie taught the small group of boys in a makeshift shelter every morning and then supervised their work in the gardens. Eliza traveled up and down the rivers and creeks by canoe, visiting the villages close to the waterways. Accompanied by her interpreter Jude, she told the people about Jesus, who died for them. She also encouraged the parents to send their children to the mission to be taught.

Gradually the number of boys at the school increased. The children arrived naked or with a scanty loincloth wrapped around them. Susie and Eliza would dig out a shirt or make a pair of shorts from the few boxes of clothes they had brought with them.

The villagers were friendly people who welcomed this God-woman and extended their simple hospitality whenever she passed through. Though she had to speak through an interpreter, she soon knew many of the villagers by name, asking about their children and giving advice regarding their ailments. She never passed by without stopping to pray with those who gathered around her, and had the joy of leading many of these people to the Lord.

Even though Eliza received warmth and acceptance from the villagers, she was horrified at some of the practices she encountered. The first time she saw a mother force hot pepper down her baby's throat, almost choking the screaming infant, she had to stop herself from grabbing the baby from the mother's arms.

"What are they doing to that baby?" she demanded.

Jude patiently explained, "They must begin giving the child 'man's food' a few days after it is born or it will not grow up to be strong and healthy. If the child drinks only mother's milk, it will remain weak."

As she went deeper into the jungle, Jude explained many different customs that disturbed Eliza. She saw infants washed in water so hot she could barely stand to touch it herself. She watched as their squirming bodies were rubbed with a white, pasty mixture that made them look like miniature clowns.

"That's to keep the devils away," explained Jude.

"What's the scar on the girl's arm?" she asked one day as she came across a young girl folding her arms across her budding breasts as she stopped to take a rest from grinding palm nuts.

"Those are scars from the bracelets she wore as an infant. They prove that her parents put jewelry on her as a baby."

Eliza shuddered to think of the painful sores that had developed as the bracelets grew too tight around the growing young arm.

But what distressed her most was the treatment of the little girls. To parents in the bush, girls represented an article of trade.

One father replied to Eliza's persistent request to send his girl to the mission, "We don't give girls away; we sell them."

"We don't give girls away; we sell them."

Tribal girls were betrothed at about seven years of age—sometimes to men many years older, who already had several wives. At the age of ten or twelve they were taken to live with the man's people to learn "his fashion."

Since the dowry was paid when the arrangement was concluded, it was considered a waste of time and effort to educate a girl who already belonged to another family. Instead, her services were utilized in the hut and garden as long as she was at home. Eliza and Susie nearly gave up hope that they would ever have a tribal girl at the mission.

Then one morning a distraught young woman arrived at BIA. Tied on her hip was a round-faced girl of about three, wrapped in typical tribal fashion with a hand-woven cloth. Eliza could barely understand the woman's excited Liberian English.

"Dis girl's mama, she goin' to kill me. She goin' to take da baby. Her papa give her to me so dat she get schoolin', but her mama don't like dat."

Calming the anxious woman, Eliza began to piece the story together.

Her name was Angeline, and she lived in Fortesville. A Bassa man had come into the town to work for her uncle and began to appreciate the benefits of civilization. After a few months on the job, he went back to his village in the hinterland, returning with his daughter.

He brought the child to Angeline since he knew she believed in helping native children, and he asked her to bring his daughter up. Angeline took the little girl, giving her the Anglicized name of Maude in place of her tribal name. She found the little one quick to learn, as well as obedient.

Several weeks after Maude was brought to Fortesville her mother arrived at the door, demanding her child. Angeline refused and quickly sent word to Maude's father about what had happened. The father was insistent that Maude stay in town to be reared in a civilized manner.

That night Maude's mother broke into the bedroom and took the little girl away, disappearing into the night before Angeline realized what had happened. As soon as the father could get away from the job, he went home to retrieve Maude. But he warned Angeline that his wife's people were angry and had threatened to steal the child again, even if they had to poison Angeline to do so.

And so Angeline came to Eliza to plead that she take Maude and bring her up as her father wished.

Eliza took the little girl in her arms, certain that God had answered her prayer and that Maude was just the first of many girls she would rescue from a hopeless future. At the time, the mother's anguish never entered her mind.

Maude was just the first of many girls she would rescue from a hopeless future.

By the end of 1915 Susie and Eliza were well-established in their ministry at BIA. The harvest from their little farm produced enough to stave off hunger, the children were learning well, and several hundred villagers had accepted Christ.

Eliza was confident that she had indeed found her life's work. Letters from home were infrequent. When news came that the steamer had stopped in Buchanan, Eliza waited impatiently for the mail to be brought to the mission. Included in the letters from her family and friends was a letter from Rev. James Kelly. She quickly opened it.

Sinking to the ground in dismay, Eliza read that the Baptist Convention of Texas had split from the National Baptists. Since

Eliza was the only missionary from Texas, she would have to be replaced by missionaries under the National Baptists. Her life-work, still in its infancy, seemed to have heard its death knell!

Eliza did the only thing she knew to do—she prayed. Many nights long after Susie was asleep under her mosquito netting, Eliza knelt beside her cot, her head buried in Mama's colorful patchwork quilt. Bewildered, disappointed, alone, she poured out her heart to her Father.

> *O Lord, you sent me here; you told me this was my life's work. The leaders of the convention have told me I must get ready to come home. But Father, I am not under their orders; I'm under yours, and I won't leave until you tell me to go.*

For many months there was no further word from the mission. Each time the steamer brought mail from America, she would hastily glance through the letters, almost fearful of seeing another from the Convention, yet longing for the suspense to be broken.

Within the year more than a thousand converts had accepted Christ in the villages.

As the months stretched on, Eliza and Susie tried to put the ominous news behind them. God was blessing their little mission. They now had fifty children in the school, including several little girls. A two-story, bamboo-and-thatch building, thirty-six-by-forty-feet, was complete. The boys lived upstairs, while the ground floor served as a classroom and dining room.

Even more thrilling to Eliza was the response to the gospel among the tribal people. Within the year more than a thousand converts had accepted Christ in the villages.

Toward the end of 1916 Eliza visited villages far upstream. She had never been this far before. Her heart was moved as she saw little children ill with fever, with no medical care available.

She arrived in one village to find the women all gathered in a hut with a woman in a difficult delivery. Though Eliza had little experience and no training, the women begged her to help. But it was too late. The exhausted young mother died in agony, and her infant with her. Eliza would never forget the wailing and the "talking" drums that throbbed through the night, sending the woman's soul back to her ancestors.

After a week in the interior, Eliza returned to the mission in a downpour. The boys beached the dugout canoe on the sandy bottom and jumped out to tug it up on the shore. The roar of the rain, falling like great waterfalls over the edge of the clouds, muted their voices so that Eliza couldn't hear what they were saying. They steadied the canoe as she stepped out into the water, her drenched skirt clinging to her thighs and trailing in the fast-moving current.

Eliza was so thoroughly soaked that she shivered as she waded to shore, carrying her sodden canvas bag of equally sodden clothes. It seemed as though she had been wet for the entire week, though the storm had begun the previous night as she slept in one of the villager's huts.

Shouting over the storm, Eliza directed the boys to take the cassavas she had bought from the natives back to their house. Clutching the Bible wrapped in oilcloth under her arm and carrying her shapeless, mudplastered shoes in the other hand, Eliza trudged up the trail to her own thatched hut. How she anticipated getting into some dry clothes.

She expected to see Susie standing in the doorway. She usually had a good meal prepared for her when she came back from her trips into the hinterland.

But there was no sign of life in the room as she pushed open the door. The heavy clouds cast a gloomy gray spell over the hut. On the rainward side, the shutters had been closed to keep out at least some of the water that insisted on running down the frame. Muddy puddles pooled on the floor below. A damp, musty smell permeated the room.

Growing accustomed to the dim light, Eliza saw Susie lying on her cot, several blankets piled on her and pulled over her head. "Not another malaria attack," groaned Eliza as she closed the door.

"Susie, it's me, Eliza. What's the matter?"

A violent spasm shook the form huddled on the bed, and Susie's wan face emerged above the covers. "I'll be all right—I came down with the fever last night, but I've run out of quinine."

Stripping off her sodden clothes, Eliza gratefully put on a dry robe and slippers and toweled her springy black hair to shake out the moisture. How thankful she was once again for the kerosene stove so she didn't have to struggle with wet wood!

Susie was grateful for the hot tea and for the quinine Eliza fished out of her wet bag. "I'm going to Buchanan tomorrow to get supplies, so I'll get more," Eliza said consolingly.

Susie seemed to feel a bit better as she listened to Eliza's enthusiastic report of her trip, and even managed to laugh as Eliza told her how she had fallen out of the canoe when it hit a hidden log in the river.

"Those boys fished me out like a wet rag," said Eliza, her infectious laughter filling the dank room.

"And what happened here at BIA while I was away?" she asked as she finished her story.

Susie recounted several problems—the boys had not been doing their work in the garden; they had run out of salt; and the workmen had come for their money but she hadn't had enough to pay them.

"Oh, yes," she added almost as an afterthought; "we had a visitor yesterday afternoon. Mr. C. Thompson George, a man from some British country in South America, passed this way. He's just come to settle in Liberia and is visiting Mr. and Mrs. Reeves in Fortesville. I guess Mr. Reeves must have told him to see what we're doing here at the mission. He seemed very nice."

Asking a few more questions about the week's activities, Eliza could see that Susie was getting tired. She urged her to go to sleep. For a long time she sat in the darkness next to her bed, praying about her growing concern for Susie's health. The malaria attacks were coming more frequently, and Eliza had a gnawing fear that her coworker would not be able to stay in Liberia much longer.

The torrential rain ceased as suddenly as it had begun. The dripping of the water running off the thatched roof was the only sound as Eliza crawled thankfully under Mama's patchwork quilt and fell asleep.

"I wonder if Susie felt like this when she was walking to Monrovia to catch the ship," Eliza heard herself saying aloud as she realized she had been lost in a reverie of remembrance. She hadn't thought of Susie for a long time. But how vividly she now recalled those agonizing weeks while Susie debated whether she could remain in Liberia.

Susie's body had been continually wracked with fever, and she had lost so much weight that she was too weak to work. It soon became obvious that God was not going to cure Susie of malaria and that she would have to leave the fever-infested country for safer climates. With no steamers coming to Bassa because of the World War, Susie decided to walk more than seventy miles to Monrovia to catch a ship for the USA.

It still brought a lump to Eliza's throat when she remembered their tearful and final farewell. But then she straightened her sagging shoulders and called to Tosnoh and Robert, "Hurry up. If Susie could do it sick with malaria, we'll make it to Monrovia too."

chapter nine

ONE BREATH FROM DEATH
(1916–1917)

he Saturday morning heat seemed more oppressive than ever as Mother Eliza dragged her tired body along. To the boys' constant whining, "When we going to be there?" she could only say, "Soon, children, soon."

But from what the villagers had told her last night, Monrovia was at least a day-and-a-half walk—that is, if they could maintain a normal pace.

Far ahead on the beach she saw a break in the sand. That meant either the shoreline turned in around another bay, or yet another river remained to be crossed!

Mother had lost track of how many rivers and streams they had navigated already. Some were sufficiently shallow to ford at low tide, and several times friendly fishermen had taken them across. But twice they were forced to swim against a heavy current. Mother feared she did not have the strength for that again. She was relieved to find that it was a wide but fairly shallow stream. The low tide would enable them to cross easily.

Eliza had a particular dread of snakes. Fortunately, they were uncommon in the saltwater near the mouth of the river. But more than once during her treks inland to villages she had felt a slimy body slither past her as she crossed a murky jungle creek. Praise God, none had ever bitten her!

The boys, eager to reach the other side, took Mother's helmet and bag with them and splashed into the cool water. Mother took off her heavy boots and tied them to her belt. Probing the river bottom with her bare foot, she searched for flat surfaces on the slippery submerged rocks.

Midstream the current was swifter than it had seemed from the shore, but as long as the water reached only to her waist, she could maintain her balance. As Mother groped for the next secure foothold, she realized she was at a drop-off where she could no longer touch bottom. "I guess I'll just have to swim after all," she said to herself and threw herself into the water.

Mother made for a rock jutting out of the water just a few yards ahead of her. Suddenly she was drawn into an eddying whirlpool, her hands and feet flaying the water. A strong undertow caught her helpless body and propelled her out to sea. The roar of the surf drowned out her cries.

"Father! Don't let me die now. Who will take care of all my children?"

As the waves closed over her head, Mother struggled with a furious determination not to let the sea overpower her. "Father!" she cried out. "Don't let me die now. Who will take care of all my children?"

Her lungs felt as though they were bursting. A swell lifted her long enough to draw in a desperate gulp of air before the waves dashed her down into the sea. Her attempts to claw her way to the surface were as useless as holding back a giant boulder from tumbling down a hill.

"Mother . . . Mother . . . Mother."

Eliza could hear the voices of children calling her from a far distance. As she turned over and opened her eyes, she saw Tosnoh and Robert bending over her, tears streaming down their faces.

"Oh, Mother, are you all right?" cried Tosnoh as he saw her eyes open. "We thought you were dead."

"We saw you being carried out to sea, and we tried to get back to help you, but the waves were too strong," Robert blurted out, hardly able to believe that Mother was still alive.

"Then a big wave picked you up and threw you back on the shore; we just pulled you away from the water so that you wouldn't get carried back again," Robert went on. "Are you really all right, Mother?"

Eliza struggled to sit up. "I'm fine, children, just fine. Let's praise the Lord for saving my life." There on the sand the three bowed their heads while Mother thanked her heavenly Father for His protective care.

"Now, boys, help Mother to her feet, and we'll be on our way. My boots will have to dry out before I can wear them again."

Soberly the two boys walked beside Mother the rest of the day, careful not to let her out of their sight. They worried about her. She seemed so quiet, lost in a daze—sometimes talking to herself, other times softly saying, "Yes, Lord; that's how it was, Lord."

For Eliza, the walk to Monrovia had turned into a battle—not between herself and the elements, but between her and her God. Once again, her mind returned to earlier days.

In all her years in Africa, Eliza had never doubted her call. Even when the mission had stopped supporting her, or when she found the buildings destroyed and the children gone, her faith remained stalwart. Her tears had always been for those who had never heard of the love of Christ. She cried over those who were hopeless in their fear of evil spirits and for the tribal children who had no opportunity to learn. But she had never wept for herself.

She had often taught her children, "Before we can get to the good things of life, we've got to enjoy some hard things." But now, nearing the end of her physical strength, Satan attacked her spiritual stamina. Eliza began to wonder whether she had made the right decision. Perhaps she should have returned to America with Susie years ago. Perhaps God had not intended a woman to stay in Africa alone.

As she plodded along, her mind began to relive one morning more than twelve years earlier. Eliza never took a new step without earnest prayer, but no decision had been as difficult as when Mr. George had asked her to marry him. Every detail of her first meeting with him stood in sharp focus in her mind. In many ways, those days were similar to these.

Mr. George had been staying with her friends, Mr. and Mrs. Reeves, in Fortesville. Eliza had walked to Fortesville that morning in 1916 to take a boat to Buchanan to get supplies. She found Mr. Reeves and his wife making arrangements to hire a boat.

Mr. Reeves, who was a Liberian congressman, called to her when he saw her approaching. "Are you going to Buchanan this morning? Why don't you come in our boat? There are only three of us."

Eliza was grateful. Sharing the cost of the boat would leave more of her dwindling resources for the things she needed for the school. No money had come from the Convention since news of the split. Besides, she enjoyed the company of Mr. and Mrs. Reeves, who had treated her like a daughter ever since her arrival in Liberia.

As Mother stepped into the boat she noticed a slight man, dressed in a dapper gray suit, sitting in front of Mrs. Reeves. His generous mustache seemed too large for his face, and the little patch of hair on top of his head looked like a rabbinical cap. But his smile was open and his eyes were warm and friendly as he greeted Eliza.

Mrs. Reeves turned to her: "Miss Davis, I'd like you to meet our houseguest, Mr. C. Thompson George. He came to call on you and Miss Taylor yesterday, but you were gone on a preaching tour."

"How do you do, Mr. George?" Eliza responded as she settled on the plank in front of Mrs. Reeves. "Miss Taylor told me of your visit. I'm so sorry I wasn't at home to welcome you to our little mission."

Mr. George reached his hand across Mrs. Reeves to acknowledge Eliza's greeting. "I'm pleased to make your acquaintance, Miss Davis. I traveled with some friends of yours on the ship coming from Liverpool through the Suez Canal. Do you remember Rev. and Mrs. Konigmaaker? They said they had been on the same ship with you from the States to Liverpool."

An animated conversation ensued as Eliza and Mr. George talked of their mutual friends. The rest of the journey downstream passed quickly as Mr. George regaled them with his travels from British Guyana to Europe and Africa.

C. Thompson George had studied medicine as a young man in Guyana, South America, but before completing his degree he left school to take a job in a bank. At forty-four years of age he learned of an opportunity to work for a Portuguese firm in East Africa.

"I always wanted to visit Africa," he explained in his high-pitched English accent, obviously enjoying the rapt attention of the two ladies and Mr. Reeves. "I took the opportunity to spend some time in Europe visiting London and Italy—places I had studied about in school."

Eliza was impressed with Mr. George's broad experience and education, so unlike blacks in her own country. In later years she explained her reaction. "You see, the English freed their slaves before the Americans did, so Mr. George had wonderful training. He had more sense than I had."

The travelers learned that Mr. George had sailed through the Suez and down the east coast of Africa, where he had worked on

a sugar plantation in Mozambique. There he became disillu-
sioned with colonial oppression as he saw the sugar growers
uproot entire villages, destroying crops and homes to clear the
land for sugar.

The end of his work for the Portuguese company came
when Mr. George went to oversee the burning and clearing of
some lands. A tearful tribal woman stood watching her half-
grown field of corn going up in flames. Hysterically she shouted
at him in her tribal tongue. One of his native assistants
explained, "She asks why you are doing
this to her when your skin and hair are the
same as hers."

The desire to be a missionary in Africa filled his heart.

Before leaving Mozambique, Mr.
George visited the grave of David Livingstone's wife. Standing at the tomb, his own
heart was overwhelmed that this white woman had sacrificed
her life for his brothers in Africa. Though Mr. George had
become a Christian as a child, he vowed to serve the Lord as he
stood at the graveside, and the desire to be a missionary in
Africa filled his heart.

"So you see, Miss Davis, I've come to Liberia to find a place
to serve God, just as you have. I'm working in Buchanan now, but
only until I can make other arrangements."

It seemed all too soon to Eliza that the boat was pulling up
to the shore in Buchanan, and the little party climbed out. Eliza
said goodbye to Mr. and Mrs. Reeves. Turning to thank Mr.
George for the interesting journey, she added, "You really should
put your adventures down in a book. In fact, you ought to visit
the United States to lecture and inspire the Negro youth of
America."

Eliza and her children hurried off to take care of her business
in town, and the morning's encounter was soon forgotten.

Two days later a messenger came from Fortesville with a letter for Eliza. An unwilling fear clutched her heart. Had Mr. and Mrs. Reeves received word from the Convention that she would have to leave BIA? Eliza took the letter into the hut where she could open it alone.

But the letter was not from Mr. and Mrs. Reeves, or even about the Convention. It was from Mr. George.

Eliza read with growing dismay:

Dear Miss Davis,
As I told you, I have selected Liberia as my field for service. There has risen in my heart an undying love for you, and this comes soliciting in return your affection in the consummation of the solemn vow at the sacred altar in the holy state of matrimony.

Your servant,
C. Thompson George

Eliza stared unseeing at the picture of himself that Mr. George had enclosed. *What have I done?* she thought. *How could he jump to such a conclusion?* She tried to recall her every word and gesture on the journey to Buchanan to see if she had given him any encouragement, but could think of nothing.

I only did what any friendly person would do, she consoled herself. *He wanted to tell us all about his adventures, and all I did was listen.*

Then she remembered her parting suggestion that he write a book and visit America. Could he possibly have interpreted those simple words of encouragement as something more?

The messenger was waiting for an answer. Eliza wanted to settle the matter then and there. She sat down at the kitchen table to draft a reply. The words would not come easily. How could she refuse him without hurting his feelings? But no, she had to make it clear that she was not interested in marriage, so he could not again mistake her friendship for something else.

In bold, clear handwriting, Eliza began:

Dear Mr. George:

Thank you for your letter which was delivered to me this morning. I am returning it together with the picture you enclosed. I feel I must explain that had I the desire to marry, I would have done so before leaving America. I didn't come here to marry. I came here to work for the salvation of the souls of these natives, and nothing will deter me from my course.

Your sister in Christ, Eliza L. Davis

That settles that! Eliza thought as the barefooted messenger boy disappeared along the trail into the jungle.

But Eliza was mistaken!

With Susie's continual bouts of malaria and the growing responsiveness of the villagers, Eliza's days were filled to over-flowing, and she soon forgot about the incident with Mr. George.

As Eliza and Susie cared for sick babies, taught in the school, and preached in the villages, the outside world and its problems seemed far away. News of the World War between England and Germany began filtering out to them, but they did not feel its impact until steamers stopped calling at Bassa ports. Mr. Reeves sent word that a German submarine had been seen off the coast of Monrovia. The war diverted food and other necessities from Liberia. On the mission the women were beginning to feel the pinch as they found basic commodities hard to get.

When her recurring malaria forced Susie to return to the USA, Eliza was alone, fully responsible for the children. Her usual resilient spirit began to break. The day Susie left, Eliza prayed:

Lord, I am all alone. Susie's gone; the Convention has deserted me. What am I to do, Lord? Who's going to take care of these children? How are you going to save these poor native souls if I have to leave this mission now?

For one of the rare times in her life, Eliza threw herself on the bed and wept in despair.

chapter ten

AN UNWELCOME LETTER

*E*liza's depression didn't last long. She was a woman of prayer. As she talked with her Father in the long night hours, He comforted her. The responsibility of the children in the school, the church, and the farm were all hers now. Added to these cares was the increasing concern about the lack of food. With the rainy season upon them in full force, they depended on the roots they had harvested earlier in the year. But fifty children, mostly boys, could eat a lot! Eliza watched with alarm as their little store of supplies diminished.

Adding to their problems, the rainy season was particularly heavy. Eliza and the children were marooned for weeks at the mission, as the creeks and rivers between BIA and Fortesville became too broad and swift to cross. At the first letup, Eliza sent the children out into the fields to look for unharvested cassavas or potatoes that had not yet rotted.

Maude had been a great comfort to Eliza, especially since Susie left, and Eliza regarded her as her own daughter. Though only about five years old—no one was sure when she was born— Maude helped with the chores on the mission just as the other children did.

This morning she was out in the garden digging to find some potatoes when she saw Father Reeves, as the children called him, coming up the path. He was the first visitor to the mission in weeks, and Maude was delighted.

Lifting her up in his strong arms, Mr. Reeves smiled and asked, "And what are you doing out here in the mud, child?"

"I'm hungry, Father Reeves, and Mother Eliza sent us all out to look for potatoes. But I can't find any." Her round little face crinkled up to cry.

Eliza later recalled how God met their needs at that desperate time.

"A note was delivered to me from Mrs. Reeves. She said she had been thinking about us during the heavy rains and was sending some rice. The boys brought the rice the next day, along with a note from Rev. Reeves that asked me to send a sufficient number of boys to the beach to bring a 100-pound bag of rice. The boys went as requested and returned with the rice and another note from Rev. Liberty of Edina that said, 'At your convenience send more boys for two bags of rice, 100 pounds each.' We prayerfully thanked God for the showers of blessings He had bestowed upon us while we were marooned in the mission by the heavy downpour of rain."

When the rains subsided, Eliza set out for Buchanan, hoping to find some gifts from the States to replenish some of the necessities they had used up. Arriving back in Fortesville, she stopped at the home of Mr. and Mrs. Reeves for a visit, glad to be with friends after the weeks of isolation on the mission. Mrs. Reeves effusively welcomed her at the door. Eliza wondered why she was making such a fuss. "Eliza, come in, come in; we have a visitor whom I'm sure will be happy to see you."

Eliza followed her down the passage to the sitting room and was taken aback to see Mr. George having tea with Mr. Reeves. Embarrassed, she hesitated before entering, but Mr. George jumped to his feet and welcomed her warmly.

"Miss Davis, I was hoping to see you on my visit here. I hear you've been having quite a time out at the mission these past months. I was so sorry to hear that Sister Taylor had to return to America."

Recovering her composure, Eliza decided that she too could act as if nothing had ever happened between them. Once again Mr. George held his audience spellbound as he told of his experiences in Buchanan in his new job.

"And, Miss Davis," he added, "I've followed your advice."

"Did I give you advice, Mr. George?" Eliza asked innocently.

"Yes, don't you remember you told me I should write down my adventures and publish them? Well, that's just what I've been doing. But I'm afraid I've run into a little problem. I have written my material out in longhand, but before I can send it away to be published, it will have to be typed. Would you know of anyone in this town who is able to type?"

Eliza hesitated. Did he know that she had taken typing at Central Texas College? Perhaps he had seen her rattly old typewriter when he visited the mission. She often left it sitting out on the table.

Before Eliza could answer, Mrs. Reeves joined in, "You type, don't you, Eliza? It would be so interesting to type a manuscript by a world traveler like Mr. George."

So Eliza returned to BIA carrying a large envelope of closely written notes, promising to let Mr. George know when she had completed the manuscript.

In spite of her personal reservations, Eliza plunged into the task with enthusiasm, finding herself avidly reading ahead in the manuscript as Mr. George unraveled his journeys around Africa. The opening pages revealed George's concern for the black people, echoing Eliza's concern for her own "bushers."

She typed:

It must be remembered that the pollution of a stream comes from its source, and any undue indifference suffered by the Negro, even when educated and civilized in all parts of the world today, is due to the glaring and undeniable fact of his brethren in Africa remaining in heathenism, indulging in habits and customs repugnant and repulsive to modern culture and civilization. . . .

It may be accounted a blessing in disguise; but to be candid, the Negro first became his own enemy in that he sold his own brethren as slaves to the white men to be transported as cattle to strange countries. . . . Today he stands wailing at oppression; oppression hard and rough, or oppression mild; a subjugate to a superior race in his own heritage. . . .

To live and breathe as a man, what is to be done by the Negro himself? There can be only one solution and answer: Let the civilized and more fortunate Negro wherever situated agitate.

Eliza felt as though he had read her mind. These were the very issues that led her to resign the position as matron in Central Texas College and come out here to this primitive land. She was even more in tune as she typed:

Increasing efforts must be put forward to enable his less fortunate brethren in Africa to be provided with churches and schools. . . . to disseminate the knowledge of the true God and His Son, our dear Lord and Savior Jesus Christ; the blessings of civilization, such as teaching thrift, industry, and economics, which could be applied and kept up by intelligent Negroes, who should feel it a pressing duty and necessity to voluntarily go forward in this great work. Those who cannot go should sustain pecuniarily and otherwise those who will.

Amen, brother, amen, thought Eliza. She wished that Mr. George could tell this to the churches that had promised to support her work in Liberia. She hadn't received any gift from some of them in over a year. Perhaps she could send a copy of the book to them so they would realize how important their help was.

> What have we as intelligent Negroes done and what are we doing for the uplifting and enlightenment of the race from which we sprung? If we have done nothing, let us begin now to do something by going or helping, for it is written, "If any provide not for his own, he is worse than an infidel."

Blowing out her candle for the night, Eliza kept thinking about the words she had typed. "Lord, you know this is the message that my people need to hear back in America. How can I get them to read these words?"

And then a thought struck her—she would ask Rev. Kelly to publish the book for the Convention. Then ministers all across the country would read it for themselves! With that exciting prospect, she fell asleep.

Mother immersed herself in her work at the mission and the progress of the manuscript. When the letter finally arrived from the Convention, it caught her by surprise. The letter from Rev. Jordan was brief and to the point.

> Rev. and Mrs. Daniel Horton will replace you at the Bible Industrial Academy. I will be accompanying them to Africa to introduce them to their new work. We will be arriving in August 1917. Please make suitable arrangements for their housing and for turning the work over to them.

Not a word about where she was to go or how she was to get there. Eliza was totally unprepared for this news.

In the weeks that followed she moved in a daze as she prepared the children for the turnover. She hugged Maude closely when she put her to bed at night, wondering what would happen to this little girl when she returned to America.

Determined to present BIA in its best light, Eliza worked from dawn till dark, urging the boys to clear the jungle farther back from the huts. The gardens were weeded and hoed meticulously. Each evening she gathered them together for prayers, but with an added fervor that they learn their memory verses word-perfect and sing their hymns without a mistake.

She continued her work on the manuscript far into the night. For those few hours she was able to lose herself in another world and forget the imminent arrival of the Hortons. Mr. George's descriptions of primitive peoples in Portuguese East Africa helped her to understand some of the enigmas of the village people with whom she worked.

> Natives of Africa as a rule have many fathers, mothers, sisters, and brothers; and to the stranger it would appear a puzzle, but can be explained in this way—grandfathers, grandmothers, uncles, and aunts are known only as fathers and mothers respectively; brothers, sisters, and cousins are known just the same as brothers and sisters, and only by close examination could the relation be solved.

Eliza nodded understandingly. That explained why Jude has a mother upstream and another down in Buchanan!

Another aspect of tribal life that troubled Eliza was the nudity. She would not allow a child to go nude on the mission, even if it meant cutting up one of the dresses in her limited wardrobe to make a shirt or skirt. Frequently she found dresses for the women who came in from the villages for medical help or to sell produce.

Mother wasn't sure what to make of Mr. George's matter-of-fact explanation of nudity:

> If any native should die in a village, there is a great lamentation among the family, all going entirely nude and sprinkled with ashes over their bodies. Extreme and absolute nudity is a show of great distress and is observed in their habits and customs irrespective of sex or who is about.

But a few pages later Eliza found herself applauding Mr. George's observations of the natives on the Portuguese island of San Thome:

> There are a few wealthy and respectable blacks in this island, the majority being British subjects from Sierra Leone, but the condition of blacks on the whole, as in all Portuguese colonies, is deplorable, for strong drink, that dread curse of nations, is sold to the natives equally as food and results in crowded jails.

Eliza had already seen enough drunkenness among the Liberians to realize that it was as great a problem here as in the southern United States. Liberian men tapped the trees to make palm wine. More than once she had delivered an impromptu sermon on the dangers of strong drink!

During these days of frantic preparation for the Hortons, Eliza received a letter from Rev. Kelly. He wished to console her over the tragic events that had forced the split. Offering a ray of hope, he suggested that she try to find another piece of land that could be used for a new mission. Once things had settled down, perhaps the Texas Convention could assume responsibility.

And so Eliza's heart was light that day, though she knew that the Liberian Baptists already cooperated with the National Baptist Convention here in Bassa County. It was unlikely that they would grant another Baptist group a mission site.

That night Eliza finished typing Mr. George's manuscript, more determined than ever to ask Rev. Kelly to publish it. But in rereading the manuscript, one section angered her. She considered asking Mr. George to eliminate it.

It was a letter from an Anglican minister who had held services onboard the *Prinz Regent*, the vessel on which Mr. George traveled up the coast of Africa. Rev. Wright had written a letter to the Church Missionary Society in London and sent a copy to Mr. George. It read in part:

> After the service I had a talk with the colored gentlemen and ladies (two had their wives with them) and learned the most interesting fact: the grandparents of these men were formerly slaves, who through the preaching of the missionaries who lived amongst them in the years gone by became Christians. When the slaves were emancipated, these, of course, obtained their freedom, and these, our fellow-passengers, their grandchildren, are sincere members of the Christian church going as missionaries of civilization back to the continent from which their forefathers were wrested as slaves.

To this point Eliza had no argument. Wasn't she herself one of these slave descendants now in Africa as a missionary to the land of her forefathers? But the letter went on:

> As we joined together in worship on other occasions, our hearts were cheered to see the results of missionary efforts in the years gone by, and we were encouraged to persevere with our work amongst these degraded Basukuma at Nassa,

78

knowing that our labor is not in vain, and that even if our few converts seem to come short of the ideal we have for them, yet we must not forget the long generations of animal existence behind them and the terribly strong hereditary tendency to vice against which they have to contend. Only after two or three generations, as in the case of our black friends on the ship, can we expect them to come up to the standard of Christian people in Europe.

Here Mother took strong exception. What was this "animal tendency to vice"? Who enslaved the Africans, beat and mistreated the slaves, and lynched free men? If there was an animal tendency in man, it certainly wasn't limited to Africans!

Eliza sent a message to Mr. George that the manuscript was completed, and the following Sunday he arrived in time for the church service. She couldn't help but feel happy to see him. As the time for the Hortons' arrival drew closer, she became more and more discouraged. It was good to talk with someone who understood.

As they went over the manuscript Eliza explained her plan to ask Rev. Kelly to publish it, and Mr. George readily consented.

"In fact, Miss Davis, I understand you have written several poems which are very good. Would you consider including one of those in the book?"

Laughing it off at first, Eliza allowed herself to be persuaded to show him the little notebook of poems and words to hymns that she had written. Looking through the notebook, Mr. George pointed out one of her favorites. "Here's the one we should use, Miss Davis. In fact, I'll try to write some music for this—I've done a little composing in the past."

And so while he sat in the wicker barrel chair by the window reading through the manuscript, Eliza typed up her creation.

Seeking the Lost
There's a great responsibility upon me;
    The Lord now bids me go.
I cannot stay but must hasten far away,
    Where the lost are dying so.

Chorus:
Seeking for the lost ones,
Praying for the lost ones,
Working for the lost daily here;
Looking unto Jesus
Amidst heathen darkness,
Seeking for the lost daily here.

There are millions lost, who are groping in the dark;
    O how dreadful is their state!
They are lost in sin; may we not now seek to win
    Those dear souls for Jesus' sake.

Do you feel relieved when the Savior is displeased?
    See these dear souls pass away.
Jesus' life paid the cost; then why should they be lost?
    Christians, help save them today!

O how sad to know that the heathen too will go
    Into judgment without grace;
Lost forever in sin, in a world that has no end—
    What a dreadful doom to face!

All are not sent to preach, but the lost we all may reach;
    God has servants on the way
Who are working night and day; help them either go or
        stay—
    Spread the gospel news today.

This was to become one of the children's favorite hymns in the years ahead as Eliza shared her burden for the lost with the students in her care.

As Mr. George started to leave for Fortesville, he turned back to Eliza. "Miss Davis, I know you have many problems on your mind right now, and this may be the wrong time to bring it up. But my desire to marry you still remains. Won't you at least promise me that you will give it further thought?"

Looking at this kindly little man, several inches shorter than she and several years older, Eliza didn't have the heart to reject him to his face. "I'll think about it, Mr. George," she promised. "I'll think about it."

chapter eleven

MOTHER ELIZA
(1917–1918)

*Y*ou'll have to watch the boys, Ora. They will waste hours on a Saturday morning gathering palm nuts if you aren't strict about how much they have to bring back before lunch." Eliza had spent days explaining the running of the mission to Daniel and Ora Horton, her replacements from America.

Tension reigned the first few days after the Hortons arrived with Dr. Jordan. But a grudging admission that Eliza and Susie had done a remarkable job in establishing BIA in such a short time lent Eliza some relief. The fifty children had been on their best behavior. Even the rains held off.

But in spite of the good impression, Dr. Jordan made it abundantly clear that the National Baptists had no commitment to Eliza. The Texas Baptist Convention was now responsible for her. He told her she could stay at BIA until the end of the year, but after that she would have to find another ministry or go home. How she was to find the fare for her return trip was up to her.

Though these had been difficult days, Eliza could not help but like the cheerful and dedicated Hortons. They were graduates of Morehouse and Spelman Colleges in the States and brought with them a wealth of experience and a love for the Liberian people. If she had to leave, Eliza could not have chosen a better couple to succeed her.

She and Ora Horton became especially close. Eliza found herself pouring out her heart to this warm and loving person. The Hortons were distressed about Eliza's future, but their hands were tied.

Night after night Eliza spent hours in prayer asking God for guidance. Even if she were to go home, she had no funds. God would have to provide passage in a miraculous way. But above all, she pleaded to stay. This was her life's work, and she had been in Africa only four years.

> Night after night Eliza spent hours in prayer asking God for guidance.

One night as she knelt beside her bed agonizing in prayer, she seemed to hear a still, small voice beside her saying, "Daughter Eliza, do not be discouraged, for I have another field of fruitful service for you. Trust Me, and I will guide you."

Praising God, she got up from her knees, confident that the God who had led her to Africa would keep her here.

In the weeks that followed, Eliza continued to work among the women and children in the villages. The outreach that she and Susie had begun among the Bassa Baptist women was bearing fruit. The women's convention was to meet in Buchanan in December, when the women were to bring in their pledges for the work of BIA.

Eliza was confident that God had assured her she could stay in Africa. But there seemed to be no answer to the problem of where and how. In the midst of this dilemma, Mr. George appeared at the mission. He announced that he was leaving for Sinoe County, some one hundred miles farther south on the Liberian coast, where he had been offered a job. There was a small settlement in Greenville and a few families several miles inland at Lexington, but outside of that it was untouched by civilization.

"Perhaps you would like to have me look for a place to start another mission," Mr. George offered. "From what I have learned from people who have been to Sinoe, there are few schools for the tribal children in the area."

Eliza's eyes grew wide as she listened to Mr. George's suggestion. She had never thought of moving to a totally new area. *That may be just the way to obtain a site, and perhaps the Baptist convention would agree to back me there,* she mused.

Then she realized that Mr. George was still talking, "Of course you know, Miss Davis, that a single woman like you could never work in such a primitive area alone. Some missions have withdrawn their missionaries from tribal areas because it is too dangerous. You would really need a man to work with you."

She looked at him with growing astonishment, afraid to anticipate his meaning.

"If you would marry me, I would be willing to leave my job and go with you to help start a new mission."

Eliza was stunned. How could he keep harping on marriage? Didn't he realize she was an old maid, almost forty, and really had little desire for marriage? And yet—could it possibly be that this was the way God was going to allow her to remain in Africa?

Confused, she wished he would just go away and permit her to think. Sensing her hesitation, C. Thompson pressed his point. "Miss Davis, I know you refused me once, but things have changed. Unless you find someone to help you, the Convention is going to force you to leave Africa. We could really work together well. You are a trained teacher with a wonderful way with the natives. I've had years of experience among them and know what it's like to exist in the rugged interior. Won't you let me go and try to find a place for a mission?"

Eliza needed time to think and pray, but Mr. George was scheduled to leave for Sinoe the next day. He pressed for an answer.

What should she do? She had given up any thought of marriage years ago. She couldn't imagine herself married to this little man who seemed so determined to have his way. But even more shattering was the thought of leaving Africa, where she so clearly felt that God had called her.

She had given up any thought of marriage years ago.

In desperation, she blurted out, "All right, Mr. George, you take my letter to the authorities requesting permission to begin work in Sinoe. And, if they agree," she heard herself saying, "I'll marry you."

In the weeks that followed Eliza vacillated between utter disbelief that she could have committed herself to such a course of action and the assurance that nothing would come of Mr. George's wild plan. *But if he fails, what do I do?* she thought.

She argued with God long into the night. "Help me, Father. You see what a confusion I'm in. Make it plain what you want me to do."

Eliza pushed her personal dilemma to the back of her mind and immersed herself in the pressing responsibilities of the mission. The Bassa Baptist Women's Convention at Buchanan was approaching, and Eliza had trained a group of BIA children to sing at the convention. How thrilled she was to see hundreds of Bassa and Americo-Liberian women meeting together for the first time!

Eliza spoke with unusual power and conviction to the women about her ministry at BIA. In the offering that followed her message, the women met their goal of $500 for BIA, and for the first time since its inception the school had a financial balance.

Toward the end of the convention, as Eliza was in her room, someone called out to her, "Miss Davis, there's a gentleman asking to see you."

Her heart leaped to her throat. Intuitively she knew it must be C. Thompson George, though she had heard nothing from him in the weeks since he had left for Sinoe.

Their meeting was strained, and Eliza tried to avoid meeting his eyes. Groping for words, she found it difficult to make small talk. But as they walked together along the beach past the wooden police station and the straggling row of houses on stilts, Mr. George, expansive as ever, told her of his trip to Sinoe.

"It's far less civilized than here. There are no roads at all into the interior from the coast. To get anywhere you just have to cut your way through the jungle and across swamps. There are dozens of tribal villages within a few miles of Greenville, but few schools or churches.

"Steamers do stop in Greenville now and again. It's a small port town and trading center for tribal people bringing their produce to market. There are a number of America-Liberian families who have settled there.

"But the Kru are still defying the government, and there is a lot of fighting going on. In fact, I heard that the Kru warriors still occasionally resort to eating their captured enemies."

Unable to restrain herself, Eliza blurted out, "Were you able to get permission for me to start a mission there, Mr. George?"

"Yes, we were able to talk with the chiefs in the area, and they have agreed to set aside seventy-five acres for a mission school. And so," Mr. George went on, "I did what you told me to do, Miss Davis."

Feigning ignorance, Eliza asked apprehensively, "And what was that, Mr. George?"

"Why, you know you told me if I came back with permission to start a mission, you would marry me, and we would go together to work in Sinoe. I brought the letter and," tapping his breast pocket, "here is the marriage license."

Eliza stopped in her tracks. "Why, Mr. George—I, ah—I'm not sure. You know I've never been married before, and now you tell me to marry you just all of a sudden like this?"

For a moment C. Thompson George lost patience and threw up his hands, sharply responding, "Look here, Miss Davis, you made the plan, I didn't. I simply did what you asked me to do."

Then, seeing her distraught face, he realized how upset she was. "I'm sorry, I didn't mean to rush you. But you did suggest I could get a marriage license if I found a place for us to work, didn't you?"

For the first time Eliza looked straight into Mr. George's face and saw the pleading look in his eye. Suddenly it all fell into place. Though she didn't love this little man with his English accent and his vast experience, she did respect and admire him. He was a fine Christian, and so intelligent. And he was offering her the only hope to remain in Africa. Yes, they could work well together. Perhaps God wanted her to be married after all.

Reaching out to touch him for the first time, Eliza put her hand on his arm and heard herself saying, "Well, all right, Mr. George. I did make the plan, and you did your part. I believe God has shown me that I should marry you."

On the 12th of January, 1918, Eliza Loretta Davis and Charles Thompson George were united in marriage at the Baptist Church in Hartsford in Bassa County. Rev. James Clark officiated.

The bride wore a white duck dress she had brought with her from America. Her only attendants were the Hortons. The matronly bride seemed dazed as she came out of the church. She wasn't quite sure all this was happening to her.

Only when the children from the mission crowded around shouting loudly and cheering, calling "Congratulations, Mother Davis!" did the reality strike her.

Stooping to hug them as they crowded around her, she said, "Now, children, you have to remember, I'm not Mother Davis anymore. From now on you'll have to call me Mother Eliza."

And she had been "Mother Eliza" or "Mother Eliza George" for more than twelve years now—twelve difficult years of struggle, but twelve good years too. "Lord," she admitted, "You kept your promise and gave me my work to do here in Sinoe. No, Lord, it was no mistake. Here's where I belong, and I would never have made it without Mr. George. Just bless him wherever he is today, and help him not to worry about us back here in Liberia." And then she added for the hundredth time that day, "And help us to get to Monrovia on time."

chapter twelve

"WHY DID YOU WAIT SO LONG?"

(1918–1919)

*M*emories continued to flood Mother Eliza's mind as she pushed her weary body onward. Her brush with death only heightened her sense of detachment. On and on she trudged, lost in the past, oblivious to her surroundings.

Mother's wedding to Mr. George had always seemed vague and unreal to her, but her "honeymoon" was indelibly painted in her mind. Within hours of the ceremony, she and Mr. George and Maude had set off for Sinoe in the only transportation available to them—a twenty-foot-long, hand-carved rowboat. The pounding surf and hidden shoals were dangerous enough. Only later did the Georges learn of an even greater menace.

On the very day of their wedding, Liberia declared war against Germany. A German submarine surfaced off Monrovia and sank the nation's only armed vessel, the *Lark*. The U-boat's officers then proceeded to the capitol and requested that all British citizens be turned over to them. When President Howard refused, the U-boat began shelling the tiny thatch-roofed capitol indiscriminately. Two people were killed.

Unaware of the international turbulence taking place only one hundred miles west of them, the Georges traveled for two days along the rugged coast. The Kru sailors, whose ancestors had been skillful seamen for hundreds of years, kept the bobbing boat under control, and Eliza had every confidence they would reach their destination.

It was strange to think of herself as a married woman. Out at sea conversation was difficult because of the wind. Eliza was grateful just to contemplate the broad backs of the Kru rowers transporting her to the next stage of her life's work. Mr. George would have to fit in as best he could.

The Georges were moving into Kru territory, occupied by the tribesmen who had been the middlemen in the slave trade. The men wore the Kru sign, a two-inch scar slashed across their foreheads. Many believed this identified them as "unsuitable" for slavery. Whatever the reason, the Kru had effectively resisted slavery while capturing and selling people from neighboring tribes.

During the early part of the twentieth century a movement of God's Spirit brought many coastal Kru into the churches—Methodist, Baptist, and Roman Catholic—though it did not affect the interior villages. Thus, when the Georges arrived, they were welcomed warmly by the three churches of Zion Grove Baptist Association of Sinoe and were invited to stay in the home of Rev. and Mrs. Amos Witherspoon in Lexington.

The settlement, a few miles inland from the port town of Greenville, could hardly be called a village. Its lone dirt trail doglegged through the forest to the river's edge. A dozen two-story thatch and zinc houses hid away in the underbrush. Several had been deserted and were reclaimed by a tangle of vines and jungle growth.

Lexington's civilized residents worked their farms or held political posts in Greenville or Monrovia. Kru fishermen worked up and down the coast, spreading their great fishing nets out to dry between the wooden stilts under the houses.

There was no store, post office, bank, clinic, manufacturer, telephone system, tarred road, office, or school in Lexington. There *were* mosquitoes, politicians, churches, ants, swamps, and heat! Round-faced children clung shyly to their mothers' brightly colored lappas as the newcomers walked by to the Witherspoons' house.

C. Thompson George had done his work well on his earlier visit, and all the people were eager for the Georges to settle in the area. Shortly after their arrival, the church leaders took the Georges up-country to meet with the chiefs and village elders to arrange for a piece of ground on which to start a mission.

Many suggested that the new work be established near Lexington, where it would be more accessible. But Eliza was adamant that they move farther inland. She wanted to be closer to the unreached tribal villages, even though it meant walking through miles of swamps to reach the mission.

> To be closer to the unreached tribal villages meant walking through miles of swamps to reach the mission.

After deliberations with the chiefs of the Sno tribe, a sub-group of the Kru, a seventy-five-acre plot was granted in the name of the General Baptist State Convention of Texas. The new mission would be built in a swampy, malaria-infested area between Maneytown and Parson Village.

While they waited in Lexington for the land to be cleared and several huts to be built, Eliza and Mr. George kept busy. They started a school in the Baptist church for the children of the town. Happily, a number of tribespeople allowed their children to attend as well.

Though only six years old, Maude demonstrated spiritual discernment far beyond her years. Mother Eliza proudly wrote in her autobiography, "At the close of school one evening, Maude had the children sing with her while she prayed for them and told them about Jesus. Many of them were converted and walked home in the rain to tell their parents that they loved Jesus and wanted to join the church and be baptized." Given the obvious receptiveness of the children, the Georges held revival meetings in the church, and seventy-five people were converted.

> "Mother Eliza never struck the children— she would spank with her mouth."

Even before the mission was ready for occupancy, the Georges decided to name it after their friend, the Rev. James Kelly. And so it became Kelton Mission. The two cone-shaped thatch huts, though primitive, were ready at last. Eliza and Mr. George gladly moved the schoolchildren out to Kelton. Eliza had to admit that it was much easier having a man to supervise the farm and discipline the children.

Years later, when those children were asked who was the strictest disciplinarian, the verdict was, "Mother Eliza never struck the children—she would spank with her mouth. But the old man, he beat us when we didn't work hard."

And hard work was essential. Funds from America came only sporadically; the Convention itself sent very little. Some of Eliza's friends, such as the Rev. S. A. Pleasant, who had been a fellow classmate at Guadalupe College, sent gifts when they could. But it was never enough. Thus it was vital that a good rice crop was harvested and that cassavas, potatoes, and other vegetables be planted.

Rice-harvesting time came none too soon in that year of 1919. The food supplies were nearly gone, and Mother Eliza found herself praying for a miracle. The children proudly brought the first basket of brown grain to her from the field, led by a boy Mr. George had named Jimmy George.

Mother Eliza soon established what was to become her practice throughout her years in Africa. The children were called together for singing and prayers three times a day no matter where they were working. Mother's strong, clear voice rang out across the station as she sang old hymns like "Jesus, Keep Me Near the Cross" in typical southern style. The children would join in as they gathered around her.

Even though Mother had thirty children on the mission to teach, feed, and discipline, she was not content to stay at Kelton. The villages upstream were more primitive and isolated than the ones she had found in Bassa, and not all of them could be reached by canoe. Taking several of the older boys with her, she hiked through the swamps, sometimes walking through water up to her chin or balancing on footbridges made of barkless poles worn slippery from use.

"How long ago did this man die for us?"

Speaking through an interpreter, Mother stopped in each village, calling the people together to tell them "about a Man who died for you."

The villagers were perplexed. "Why did He die for us? We don't even know Him."

Mother explained patiently that Jesus died so that they could go to heaven, but that they must believe in Him and stop fearing the "country devil."

Sometimes the villagers asked, "How long ago did this man die for us?"

And she had to respond, "Oh, a long, long time ago."

Then they scratched their heads and complained, "How come you are just coming to tell us this now? Our mothers and brothers and fathers have died, and they didn't know about this. How come you tell us now?"

It was as though her vision in Texas of Africans streaming past the judgment seat were coming true. With a heavy heart she had to admit that these unreached people had a right to ask that question.

The urgency of telling the villagers about Jesus drove Mother Eliza day after day, even when malaria began to wrack her body and huge sores developed on her legs from wading through the swamps. Though she took her quinine faithfully, it was not always effective. When she could ignore the debilitating fever no longer, she took to her bed while Father George supervised the children.

Many of the village chiefs became her friends and were honored to welcome her into their huts. Old man Maney, chief of the nearest village, often came to visit Mother and Father George, sometimes bringing his whole contingent of wives. Mother reprimanded him, "Maney, you've got too many wives. You should give up some of them, and give your heart to Jesus."

But old Maney grinned his toothless grin, saying, "Mama, you see me. I'm old. My wives are my glory. But I'll tell you what I'm going to do. I'll give you all my children and let them trust in your God."

Shaking his head, he went on sadly, "If I'd give away my wives now, I'd be made ashamed."

But eventually, Maney agreed to give up his wives and accept the Lord.

As 1919 drew to a close, the world seemed to move in on Mother. She had been in Africa six years. The heat, fever, hunger, and hard work were exacting a toll. As she wrote to friends in Texas, they read between the lines that perhaps it was time for her to come home for a rest. Mrs. M. A. Fuller, the corresponding secretary of the Women's Auxiliary of the Convention, encouraged several of the pastors to raise funds for Mother and Maude to return to the USA.

Toward the end of the year Father George made a trip into Greenville to pick up the mail for the mission. He returned to find Mother Eliza once again down with a malaria attack.

"Eldie," he called as he came into the hut, "I have good news for you. Your friends in Texas have sent enough money for you and Maudie to go back home for awhile." There was a strange sound to his voice, and he walked unsteadily across the floor as he brought Mother the mail.

For a moment Mother wondered if he was also coming down with a fever. But when he bent over to kiss her the reason was clear.

Eliza did not find the physical intimacies of marriage easy. She always attributed this to the fact that she had been an "old maid" when she married. But to have her husband smell of liquor repulsed her.

Pushing him away, she sat up in bed. "C. Thompson George, you've been drinking. What in the world has happened to you— a minister of God and responsible for all these native children!" The anguish in those deep-set brown eyes, ringed with fatigue and fever, touched George more than her accusing words. He had meant to bluff his way through, as he had been able to do for years in the past, but he couldn't.

"I'm sorry, Eldie, it won't happen again. Sometimes I get so worried about you and where we're going to get money to feed all these children, and in a moment of weakness I accept a drink. I guess it comes from all those years tramping around Africa myself, living with godless men. But I promise you I won't do it anymore. Pray for me, Eldie, pray for me."

chapter thirteen

THE LONG HOMECOMING

(1920–1928)

I been prayin', I been prayin'," Mother mumbled aloud. Startled, the boys asked her what she was talking about, but she didn't seem to hear them.

It was obvious to Tosnoh and Robert that Mother was ill. Though they had hoped to push on to Monrovia by nightfall, they began to look for a village so she could rest.

Robert offered Mother a drink from their precious water supply. Her hand trembled as she lifted the cup to her mouth. "You go look for a place where she can lie down, Tosnoh," Robert instructed, "and I'll stay with Mother." Taking her hot, dry hand in his, he gently pulled her along under the relentless sun. Fear clutched his heart. He couldn't remember Mother being so sick before.

By midafternoon Tosnoh had found a village a few yards into the jungle from the beach. They led Mother to the chief's house, where she was offered a mat and a meal.

But to Eliza's confused and feverish mind, she was coming home. She imagined that it was eight years earlier, 1920, and Mama and Papa were waiting for her with arms outstretched. How they had missed her these seven years since she first left home! How proud they were of their "missionary daughter"—the first black missionary woman to go from Texas!

During Eliza's first visit home, the trip had taken five-and-a-half months! She had spent the first several months in Monrovia so she could adopt Maude and plow through the endless paper-work necessary to take her to America. While in Monrovia they met the Hortons, who were in the capitol for a rest, and they caught up on all the news from BIA. The couple told her that the mission was moving them to Monrovia at the end of their term. Mother promised to visit them on her way back from America.

Upon arriving in America, her family wanted to hear every detail of her experiences. She kept them all spellbound as she told them of her life in the bush. They whooped with laughter as she recounted the smaller troubles in her dramatic way they knew so well. They shook their heads in sympathy as she told of sick babies and hapless third and fourth wives quarreling in the villages.

Mama and Papa looked more wrinkled and bent, but the loving sparkle in their eyes was proof of their joy at her return. Jenny Belle had married and been widowed while she was away. Other members of the family had moved out to establish their own homes. But they were all together now, and it seemed as though little had changed in the clapboard house in Tyler, Texas.

The nation, emerging from the war years, was enjoying a technological boom. When Eliza had left America in 1914, the automobile was still the toy of the rich. When she returned in 1920, Mr. Ford's clone was everywhere. Road builders were unable to keep pace with auto production. Electric lights glistened in many homes, radiograms blared, and movie theaters attracted fun-seeking crowds.

Some of the changes shocked Eliza's Victorian spirit—the suffragettes, the flappers, the bootlegging. It saddened her to come back to the racial prejudices and tensions in her own land and to realize that the Ku Klux Klan was now more powerful than when she had left.

But to eight-year-old Maude, America was a wonder world of fantasy never imagined back on the Pepper Coast. She bounced endlessly on the soft chairs; she squealed with delight when Eliza put her hand on the ice block in the icebox; she pressed her fat little face against the window panes that kept out the rain without darkening the room.

It was good to get home to her family, but Mother was soon homesick for Africa. She was anxious to know how her husband was getting along back at Kelton. Mr. George had stayed behind to build a more durable house for them. Their mud-and-thatch hut was already showing signs of disintegration.

> **Mother was soon homesick for Africa.**

Eliza hoped to send him money for the building soon. But she was beginning to realize that it might take her several years to raise the funds to return. Though the country was prosperous after the war, blacks earned very little. Many African-American Christians were very interested in the work in Liberia and gave what they could, but most found it difficult to contribute. It was hard to sympathize with the needs in faraway Africa when their own financial and social problems were so pressing. In fact, many envied the apparent freedom and security of their African sisters and brothers, and were unable to comprehend the fear and bondage of living under heathen tribal religions.

Eliza had been home almost two years when she received a letter from her husband telling her that his money was gone. He could no longer work on the house and asked her to send him sufficient funds so he could join her in the States. They could visit churches together to raise money. Dutifully Eliza took her savings and sent it to Mr. George.

Sea travel in the twenties was slow and unpredictable, and Eliza did not expect to see Mr. George for at least six months. Few ships came directly from Monrovia to America. It was difficult to make connections without long layovers.

Taking a Spanish steamer to Mexico, Mr. George was delayed by immigration authorities for six months. When Eliza learned of his predicament, she wrote to Dr. Frank, chairman of the National Foreign Mission Board, the breakaway group to which the Texas Convention belonged. But Dr. Frank replied that there was nothing he could do.

Mother was at her wits' end. She had sent Mr. George funds in Mexico so he could maintain himself there, but her own resources were rapidly diminishing. She was no closer to returning to Africa than when she had first arrived. Finally Mama came up with a suggestion: "Daughter, I think you should ask the advice of the white Baptist minister in town, Dr. Jester. He's so friendly and nice. And you know, white folks seem to be able to take care of such things."

Accustomed to the Jim Crow South, Eliza had little contact with white churches. But, willing to try anything to bring the impasse to an end, she contacted Dr. Jester. He wrote the immigration department in Washington and obtained permission for Mr. George to enter the USA.

Eliza never spoke of her family's impressions of Mr. George, and very few of her friends ever recall meeting him. But the Georges did spend most of 1923 traveling from church to church, presenting the work in Liberia. Rev. George, as he was called by now, shared in the meetings, but it was Mother's dramatic storytelling and implicit faith in God that won them many friends. And little Maude warmed her way into countless hearts as she told them how she loved Jesus.

Eliza was most concerned for the children back in Kelton. She quizzed her husband until she knew what had happened to each one. Most of them she had sent back to their parents when she left. A few years break in their education would make little difference, since most of them would never have gone to school at all without Mother Eliza. They could easily resume their studies when she returned.

Father George informed her that a few of the boys, including Jimmy George, who had no parents, had remained at Kelton. He had arranged for a woman from the village to care for them.

The Georges spent many hours discussing their financial situation. It would be so much easier if the National Baptists would support their work regularly; instead, they had to depend on sporadic gifts from interested friends. Mother and Rev. George traveled to Louisville, Kentucky, to see Dr. Frank, hoping that an agreement could be reached. But though the work at Kelton now fell under the National Baptist jurisdiction, no funds were available.

"You'll just have to go out there and help yourselves," Dr. Frank told them.

By now, Mr. George's visa was about to expire. Crestfallen, the couple returned to Houston to their faithful friend, Dr. S. A. Pleasant, moderator of the Mount Zion district. Listening to their discouraging report, Rev. Pleasant agreed to help. He contacted the ministers of the other churches in the district and told them of the Georges' situation. In the remaining weeks before Mr. George was to sail, the churches gave enough to provide not only his fare, but to purchase carpentry tools, farming implements, and other necessities for the mission.

Since there were other churches in the district still to visit, Eliza agreed to remain behind to raise more funds. How she longed to sail with Mr. George, to get back to her beloved native children and the tribal villages that did not have the gospel!

She waited eagerly for word from Mr. George about the children left behind at Kelton and about her friends and converts in Lexington. When his letter finally came, there was disappointingly little news except to say that all the children had left the mission. But he did urge her to hurry back. He needed window frames and other building materials he could not get in Liberia. He wanted her to purchase them in Hamburg and would meet her there. They could travel back to Liberia together.

The plan sounded strange to Mother Eliza. Since there was no time to exchange correspondence, she hastily made arrangements to sail, holding meetings wherever she could as she moved eastward across the country.

But in Louisville her plans fell to pieces. Mother became ill and missed the steamer out of New York. There was no way to let Mr. George know, for he was already on his way.

The disappointments and irritations that had compounded on this furlough would have broken a lesser woman. Mother had now been in the USA for six years trying to raise money. The mission in Africa was closed and the children were scattered. The mission board under whom she served showed only halfhearted interest in her work and gave little support. She was forty-six years old, ailing, and married to a man she didn't understand. Yet she remained determined to return to Africa.

When she didn't appear in Hamburg, Rev. George used the money she had sent for building materials and sailed to America to find his wife. After they were reunited, Eliza's physical condition slowly improved, and the two began to hold meetings in Kansas. But her trials were not over—before the end of 1926 she had to have major surgery. A few months later her mother passed away. Then her husband's visa ran out, and he had to go to Cuba so he could reenter the USA on a new quota.

With traveling and medical expenses, their money was nearly depleted. As soon as Eliza was strong enough, the Georges resumed traveling. There were many opportunities to speak in black churches in Kentucky, Kansas, Nebraska, and especially Texas. Though few pledged to send support regularly, the people responded warmly, and the Georges felt they had developed a strong base.

The couple held their last meeting at the St. John's Baptist Church in Houston, home of the godly group of people led by Dr. Pleasant, who had come to their rescue so many times before. It had now been eight years since Eliza and Maude had left Liberia—eight years of struggle, disappointment, sorrow, and hardship. Maude was now a young lady of sixteen. Mother Eliza often wondered if she would ever return to her beloved Africa, but she never succumbed to the temptation to give up. God had called her to serve Him in Liberia. She clung tenaciously to that conviction until the day they boarded the ship sailing east to the Pepper Coast.

chapter fourteen

A SUDDEN HUSH

(1928–1929)

All through the night Tosnoh and Robert could hear Mother tossing and talking, sometimes to her Mama and Papa, sometimes to Maude.

"You've been a good girl, Maude. You have been such a help taking care of the little children. Why, I could never have taken care of Cerella without you," she mumbled before drifting off into a troubled sleep.

The boys had heard the story of Cerella many times. They had been there when Maude returned from a village one Sunday morning with the thin, sickly-looking baby girl. The baby's mother wanted her to be brought up on the mission. She had given birth to many children, but none had lived long enough even to walk. The country doctor could never help her. Every one of them had died.

Mother's heart was overjoyed when Maude brought the baby to Kelton. Though she cared for several girls whose parents were Americo-Liberians, few tribal parents saw the need of educating their daughters.

The boys often heard Mother complain that girls were treated like property. Their dowries were worth more than forty dollars in goods—goats, brass kettles, and pots. Every little girl in the village was spoken for long before she reached puberty.

Mother often tried to redeem the girls by repaying the dowry for them but was usually unsuccessful.

But now a mother had brought a baby girl to be raised at the mission! Mother Eliza named her Cerella. Under her watchful eye and loving care she grew into a chubby, cheerful little girl. Cerella was soon the center of attention for all the children on the mission. She never lacked for loving arms and playful care. Everywhere the children went, whether at work or play, Cerella was taken along.

In December, 1928, another little girl joined them. Mother had formed a choir on the mission, and took the children to Lexington to perform in a Christmas program at the Baptist church. At the time, Cecelia was visiting her grandmother in Lexington. When she heard the mission children sing, she longed to go to the mission too. But her father had disappeared, leaving her mother to raise a large family, and there was no hope for Cecelia to go to school.

As she heard Mother Eliza tell about the school at Kelton, Cecelia thought, *I would love to listen to her every day in school and help her work around the mission.*

On the way home after the program, Cecelia asked her grandmother what she had to do to live on the mission with Mother Eliza. Her grandmother replied, "I guess you just have to ask her if she'll take you, child. Are you wanting to go and stay with her?"

"Oh, yes, Grandma—I would be so good and do everything to help her. Do you think she'd take me?"

And so it was that early in 1929 Cecelia joined the group of little girls who shared Mother Eliza's two-room hut. She shadowed her idol and listened adoringly to all she had to say. The next time Mother Eliza took a group of children back to Lexington to be baptized by Rev. Birch, Cecelia was among those who had given her heart to Jesus.

Mother had a unique way of including the children in every part of her life. If there were financial needs, she would tell them about the need and say, "Children, let's pray. God will meet our need."

When she went to preach in the villages, she took as many children as she could fit in the boat. Skimming along in the canoe that took them up and down the

> "Children, let's pray. God will meet our need."

Sinoe River, Mother taught them Bible verses and hymns. To this day many of those children recall the joy of pulling on the oars while singing heartily at the top of their voices, with Mother sitting erect in the stern, clapping her hands as her clear, strong voice rose above them all.

Mother never walked to Greenville for supplies without a troupe of four or five children accompanying her. She talked to them as if they were little grownups, teaching them all along the way. The journeys always took longer than expected, for when Mother came to a village she would turn in and call the people together for a Bible lesson and prayer.

Sometimes she would tell the children Bible stories, gesturing with her walking stick and dramatizing exciting events so that they would end up standing in a huddle in the middle of the path, wide-eyed and intense, waiting for the dramatic outcome.

If they met another traveler on the path, Mother would stop and talk. She was genuinely interested in his welfare and never went on without putting her hand on his shoulder with the words, "Son, let's pray."

When she worked in the garden she set the pace, hoeing longer and faster than even the strongest boy. She never asked them to do a task twice; rather, her children embarrassingly tell how she would pick up the bucket herself and say loudly as she walked toward the river, "Well, then, Mother will get the water."

That would set off a scramble to retrieve the bucket from her. It was unthinkable to let Mother get water herself!

They remember her ingenuity as well. One of her girls, Genevieve, recalls how she cared for her clothes. "The mission girls washed her clothes, but she never worried us to press them. She would fold them up and put them on the chair. When she was writing letters at night, she would sit on the clothes and put them on in the morning."

Eliza never totally gave in to the heat of Liberia, and continued to wear the modest dress she was accustomed to back in America. The girls who washed her clothes were astounded at the "singlet"—the all-in-one romper she wore under her slip.

Despite the constant lack of funds, the limited diet, and the primitive living conditions, a pleasant spirit thrived on the mission. Mother's infectious personality and abiding faith in God established the climate.

With all there was to do and no one else to help her, Mother's teaching time was limited. The children learned the barest rudiments academically. But Kelton Mission was one big classroom in Christian living, with regular tests to ensure progress.

Kelton Mission was one big classroom in Christian living.

One such test came on a sunny day in late 1929. Mother sent Maude out to the furthest rice field to work with some of the older boys while she and the younger children prepared palm oil. As usual, Maude took Cerella on her back so that there would be no danger of her crawling about, pulling over basins and getting too close to the fire.

Suddenly Mother could hear the rush of feet and excited calls coming from the field. She jumped up to see the children running back to the mission. As they got closer she could see that the girls were crying and shouting. Panic surged over her as she noted that Maude did not have Cerella on her back.

"She's gone, Mother. The chief and some of the villagers came and took Cerella back. They said they've changed their minds, and they don't want her to stay on the mission." Maude fell to the ground, wailing hysterically, the others loudly joining in, as if in a tribal death watch.

The commotion and wailing brought the rest of the children running to see what had happened. In a few moments a crowd of bewildered and frightened youngsters surrounded Mother. They may have been "children" to her, but many of the older boys, like Robert and Tosnoh, were almost young men. Mother realized she would have to calm down these potential warriors.

"Children, let's pray."

Hearing the words they had heard every day since they had come to the mission, a sudden hush came over the distraught group as Mother committed yet another crisis to her only Source of help.

"Now you go back to the garden and finish what you were doing," she instructed the children. "Mother will fast and pray for Cerella." Her peaceful acceptance came only from her confidence in God. She knew that Cerella's abduction must have been with the advice and backing of the chief of the village. It would be difficult to persuade him to return her.

Not only had Mother Eliza grown to love Cerella as her own daughter, she knew there was no hope for her back in the village. She had watched Cerella develop from a sickly infant near death to a robust, healthy child. But in the village she would be sold for the price of the dowry to a much older man. If she were fortunate he would treat her kindly, but, as was often the case, she would be just one more slave among his other hard-working wives. She would have no opportunity to go school or to learn about Jesus as her Savior.

The boys remembered how Mother fasted and prayed for days. She did this whenever a special need arose on the mission. These days there was little to eat. The produce from the garden had been used up, and there had been no funds from overseas in months. All her sources of credit in Greenville had been exhausted. Mother owed money to every shopkeeper in town.

So the children ate potato greens cooked in palm oil or chewed the thin layer of meat around the palm nut kernel for a bit of nourishment. But Mother denied herself even that sustenance as she prayed for funds to buy Cerella back.

One morning a man from the village appeared on the mission. He looked frightened as Mother came out of her hut, calling for an interpreter.

"Sit down, son," Mother urged as she pulled a rough bench in front of the hut into the shade. "Have you brought news of Cerella?" Curious children began to lurk within hearing distance.

The man told his story in the rapid nasal Kru that Mother could not fully follow, though as she saw the children's faces break into uncontrolled grins, she realized the news was good. Robert interpreted for her. "He says he comes from Cerella's parents' village." Mother nodded impatiently.

"He says Cerella's parents saw how strong and healthy she was, and they knew she would bring a good dowry. None of their other children had lived this long, and they have not been able to receive payments of dowry to help them get the things they need. So they urged the chief to bring Cerella back to the village. He did not want to do that. He said the village had asked you to take Cerella and bring her up and that there would be trouble if he went back on his word."

Mother interjected, "He's right, you know; he shouldn't have broken his word."

Robert continued, "But at last Cerella's parents convinced the chief to give them permission, and they decided to watch for a time when Cerella was away from the mission and out of your sight. That's when they grabbed her and took her back to the village.

"But that very day the chief took sick. Nothing our country doctors did would help him, and he got worse and worse. When he died, the villagers called the witchdoctor to find out why the chief had died, and he says it's because he allowed Cerella to be stolen away from you, and that we must give her back. I've come to tell you that you can have her back."

Robert remembered how happy they had all been when Cerella returned to the mission. But now, as he watched Mother toss and turn in her delirium, he wondered if Cerella would ever see her again.

chapter fifteen

NEW STRENGTH—AND FRESH SORROW

*I*n the morning Robert was awakened by Mother shaking his shoulder vigorously. "Wake up, Robert!" she urged. "We have only a few hours to reach Monrovia. The chief says he'll take us across the last river in his boat. We can easily walk the rest of the way."

Mother stood before him looking refreshed and strong, her fever and delirium gone. Robert couldn't believe his eyes. *No wonder the natives call her God-woman,* he thought. *I've never seen such a strong woman in my life.*

The boys scrambled out of the hut after her to begin their sixth day's walk on the beach. Yesterday's trauma was soon forgotten, as signs of civilization began to appear along the shore. The villages were closer together now, and here and there the three travelers met other people walking the beaches too.

A special healing touch had revitalized Mother not only physically but mentally as well. She seemed like her old self as she talked to the boys, who still hovered over her nonetheless. Mother thanked them for their help and concern, adding how much easier it was at the mission now that some of the children were old enough to take responsibilities.

"You know, for awhile Jimmy George was the only boy Mr. George and I could count on. He's turned out to be a pretty fair carpenter."

Then, stopping to put her hand on Robert's shoulder, she added, "But I always get worried to see you children grow up and start loving girls." Seeing the boys' startled expressions, she quickly assured them, "No, I don't mean you've been loving girls, but Jimmy wasn't much older than you are when he started disappearing from the mission at night."

With her hand still on Robert's shoulder, she went on, "One night I caught him leaving, and I just stopped him and said, 'Jimmy, do you have a woman out there in one of the villages?'

"Well, Jimmy was embarrassed. He knew how I felt about keeping himself pure until he was married. It's not that Mother doesn't understand. I know what it's like in the villages—all the children running naked until they show signs of growing up; everyone sleeping in the same room, and Mother and Daddy having to make love secretly after the children are asleep.

"I've also told the chiefs that it isn't good to let all the older boys and girls in the village sleep in the same hut. They tell me that there is always someone there to supervise because they don't want the young folks getting into mischief either, but you know that doesn't work. The temptation is there to satisfy that strong natural desire. But God doesn't want you to make love with a girl until you marry her.

"Jimmy knew that, and he tried to explain what happened. It was our fault for leaving him alone here on the mission when we went to the United States. The woman that Father George left in charge didn't stay long, and pretty soon it was just a few young boys to find their own food and care for themselves. So when the other boys went away, Jimmy told me he just went out and looked for a woman.

"I tried to get that woman to marry Jimmy. I sent for her, and when she came to see me, I told her what the Bible says about marriage. I told her kindly, 'Daughter, he's my son; I raised him from small, small. I raised him to be a good Christian, not to live with a woman without marrying. Why won't you marry him?'

"But she just looked at me angrily and said, 'He's just a small boy—he's younger than I am. I can't marry him.'

"Now, boys, you remember what Mother tells you—God doesn't want you to live with a woman until you're married. You pray and ask God to help you resist temptation. When you're old enough, Mother will help you find a nice young miss to marry."

The boys had heard Mother talk like this many times, but they were so relieved to see her back to her old self again that they listened attentively and assured her that they would stay pure.

As the day wore on, the weariness of the week began to engulf them. They kept going by sheer force of will. By the time they reached the first row of houses on the edge of Monrovia, candles were flickering in the windows, and people were sitting outside around the doorways enjoying a small respite from the day's heat.

"Now, boys, you remember what Mother tells you."

Though the Hortons were never forewarned of Mother's coming, whenever they saw her walking up the path to their rambling, two-story wooden house, the entire family would rush out to greet their beloved friend. But on this Sunday night they did not see her until she staggered up the steps to the veranda. She might have collapsed had not Ora Horton reached out to grab her.

Shocked by Mother's emaciated appearance, Ora hustled her up to bed, shouting instructions that the boys be given something to eat before giving them water to wash. Ora tenderly bathed Mother's blistered and bleeding feet and treated them with one of her homemade remedies before wrapping them in soft bandages. "Eliza, what have you done to yourself?" she chided as she helped her into clean nightclothes and brushed her hair, stiff with sand and salt.

The two old friends talked for a few minutes, but Ora could see that Eliza was too exhausted to stay awake. Pulling the covers up over her, she said comfortingly, "Now you go to sleep. I'll see to the boys downstairs, and we can talk in the morning."

But Eliza half rose from the bed as she called after her departing friend, "Dearie, wake me up at daybreak—there's a steamer leaving for Sinoe tomorrow morning at ten, and I must get to the post office before then, or else this long trip will have been wasted."

The wooden post office with its rickety steps leading to the second floor sat along the only asphalt road in Monrovia. Since there were very few cars in Liberia in 1930, vendors used the street to display their wares—cassavas piled high in enamel basins, colorful lengths of cloth draped over poles, fat green plantains, and mangoes. Pedestrians milled about the street visiting shops near the waterfront—the big wooden stores of the English, German, and Dutch companies, and the small huts of the Syrians. A few telephone poles tilted dangerously along the main street and out toward the one motor road leading to the Firestone Rubber Plantation, but there was no telephone service.

Eliza and the boys stood on the wooden veranda of the post office waiting for the doors to open. Ora had provided fresh stockings to keep Mother's boots from rubbing, but Tosnoh's bare, blistered feet were swollen and sore, and even the four-mile walk from the Hortons' home to the post office had been difficult. Fortunately, the landing area for the steamer, which they were planning to board by ten o'clock, was not far away.

When Eliza reached the counter, she thrust the notification of the postal orders into the hands of the clerk. "Daughter, we must get this money cashed right away so we can take the steamer back to Sinoe this morning. Be a sweet child, and take care of it as fast as you can for Mother."

Mother had a way of charming people so that they helped her in spite of themselves, and even the methodical clerk behind the counter seemed eager to respond to Mother's pressing request. She pulled a smudged and thumbworn folder from under the counter and began checking through the shuffle of papers that seemed to be in no particular order. Meticulously she checked the number on Mother's notice with each dog-eared paper while Mother's anxiety mounted.

When she reached the bottom of the folder, the girl tried to reassure Mother, "It's probably stuck to something else—I'll go through them again."

After another fruitless search she called to a clerk who had just come to work, asking if she had seen the postal orders for Mrs. Eliza Davis George.

The young clerk languidly ambled over to the counter, tiny drops of perspiration glistening on her honey-colored skin.

"Don't you remember? That's the one that was lying around here for months, and nobody came to cash it. I sent it back to New York on the steamer last week."

> They made the 200-mile journey back to Kelton by ankle express.

Tosnoh broke down at the post office, refusing to return by way of the beach. Mother finally allowed him to remain in Monrovia to seek out a relative who had a job in the city. But Robert would not desert her. Together they made the 200-mile journey back to Kelton by ankle express. The trek was a blurred agony of hopelessness, pain, and dogged weariness that made every step a monumental effort.

Years later Eliza described the hell of those days matter-of-factly: "We walked all day until about two o'clock the next morning. My feet were blistered so badly that we stopped at a civilized place on the coast and were permitted to rest on the porch.

"The next day we walked until about nine o'clock that night. My boots were entirely worn out by this time, and by chance we came to a house out in the woods. I was unable to take another step."

Mental and physical exhaustion had finally overtaken her indomitable spirit. Eliza and Robert stayed at the house for the whole next day. What guardian angels ministered to them, who came to their rescue and organized a hammock for her to be carried to the sea, perhaps even Eliza herself did not know. It seems that by now utter exhaustion and exposure to the searing tropical heat gave those days a dreamlike quality, and its pain, like childbirth, was later mercifully forgotten.

Finally defeated, Mother borrowed $9.60 from a Mr. Dingwall to hire a canoe to take them down the coast to the mission.

In the end, Mother's usual optimism and faith prevailed. In her autobiography she recorded her return.

"We returned to Kelton. Maude was sick but cheerful. She told me how the Lord had blessed the boys to obtain deer meat given to them by some hunters.

"The Lord then blessed us by providing us with a good revival among the mission children. Most of them were happily converted. The boys cleared land and planted enough rice to keep hunger away."

Though many of her children tell of the walk to Monrovia and the devastating disappointment that awaited Mother Eliza when she got there, no one recalls that the money ever arrived. But Mother's courageous ministry in Kelton among the Kru villagers went on.

chapter sixteen

A CANNIBAL'S SON

*J*ust nine miles north of Kelton, in the tribal village of Seedor, another drama was unfolding. Though Mother did not know it at the time, Kelton Mission was changing the lives of people who had never met her. Doh's was one such life—a life that would help Mother forget the bitter disappointment of the "wasted" hike to Monrovia.

Doh's remarkable story would greatly affect her ministry for years to come. He shares that story here:

My parents tell me they had given me up for dead. My thin little body was covered with boils from head to foot, and I cried day and night in spite of everything my mother tried to do for me.

My mother, Nyonobe, blamed herself. Hadn't she foolishly gone to the fields to harvest cassava when her time was near, instead of staying close to the washhouse, where any decent woman should deliver?

Nyonobe had sensibly delivered her first two sons in the thatch washhouse, squatting on the dirt floor with the rest of the village women standing around to give emotional support. No man had had to come near to help in the final thrusts of body, which forced a man-child onto the wet ground. No sound issued from her lips. And when the afterbirth finally came forth, the women cheered and danced to announce the joyous news.

But when I was born, Nyonobe was in the cassava field. There was no time to cover her body with mud to keep her cool during the long deliv-

ery. Only Nyonnohtien, my father's second wife, was there to help as she labored in the hot, dusty field. When I was finally delivered, she named me Gbatoe, which means "cassava" — and from that disgraceful beginning, nothing went right.

My father, Marwieh, was even then a very old man — he had had many children before he was married; but in his later years, when his traveling days were over, he settled down with three wives. Nyonobe, the first and the youngest, was his favorite. She was the daughter of royalty. Her grandfather had been Wale Wohjolo. He was a "Klosla," or royal peacemaker.

The story of the origin of the Klosla had been passed from generation to generation, dating back a thousand years or more. But every child in our tribe had heard of the two brothers, Saydee and Gidikan, who had fought each other and nearly annihilated the tribe, until one of the villagers suggested that they stop fighting and make the loser serve as slave of the winner.

The villagers hailed this wise one as a peacemaker. From that time forward his descendants were known as Klosla and were revered wherever they went. No one would dare lift a finger to fight another person if the Klosla sent his three-headed staff. It was as binding as the law of the Medes and the Persians.

My grandmother, Dehwlo, was Wale's favorite daughter, and even after she married my grandfather, the village would make special preparations whenever she came home to visit her father. Every household would bring out their wooden eating bowls and form stepping stones with them to the edge of the village so that her feet did not have to touch the ground.

In those days our tribe was wealthy. When they were first married, my father, Marwieh, had been able to care for my mother well. After all, he had been the first in the tribe to deal with white people, and the first to bring cloth to the village so that the women did not have to pound the bark of trees to make skirts. Marwieh had organized crews of tribesmen to go to the coast to work on ships which traveled to such far-off places as Angola and the Congo, and he brought back exotic things from the civilized world.

I can still remember my father telling me the stories that his father told him about tribal wars. "Gbatoe, those were the days," he would tell me with a sparkle in his eyes. "My father was a great warrior, and he was usually given the opportunity to bring home the body of an enemy. But he was very fair—when the body was cut up, he made sure that every warrior was given a piece, for to eat human flesh was the best way to stay strong." He told me that Grandfather wasn't really supposed to give him any, for he was still too young to fight, but he wanted him to be a warrior too, and so he would give him a bite or two of human flesh. He liked the palms of the hands best; they were more greasy than other parts.

But when the war between our tribe and the government force started, those good days came to an end. The soldiers killed many of the villagers and destroyed our fields. The villagers fled, some to the coast and some to other areas, for our area was placed under martial law.

Life at the coast in Seedor was much more difficult, especially since my father, Marwieh, was now so old he could no longer work as hard as before. Many a day he just sat in front of the hut, watching his children play or talking with the other men in the villages. After I was born and became very sick, they spent their time discussing what had caused this strange illness in the Marwiehs' baby son.

After hours of discussion, the man finally agreed to call the witch doctor to diagnose my trouble—a measure taken only as a last resort. The witch doctor charged high fees for his services.

Of course I don't remember when he came to the village, but my mother often told me later how I screamed when I saw his face, painted with white and brown stripes, with red circles around his eyes. He was covered from his shoulders to his ankles with a grass skirt and had rows of beads hanging across his chest.

The solution was really very simple. He said, "Your son, Doh, who died last year, is angry with you, Marwieh, for not being there when he died. He has come back to trouble you in the form of this child. You must change his name from Gbatoe to Doh in order to appease his spirit." And then he gave my father a special ju-ju to hang above the door of our house to keep the spirit from entering.

My mother, Nyonobe, told me that after they began calling me Doh my boils began to go away. "It was worth the three chickens the witch doctor asked for his fee to have you healthy and happy again."

I don't really understand much about these superstitions, but I used to wonder if I wouldn't have gotten better even without the witch doctor's visit. There was no one to tell us about a better way in those days. We were only nine miles from Kelton mission, but it might as well have been ninety miles, for we were isolated and cut off from the rest of the world at Seedor.

Then in 1932, when I was four years old, my father decided that we should go back home to Shaw, for the war in the interior had ended and news had come that the tribes in that area were living in peace once again. The whole village made the forty-mile walk through the jungle and swamp. It took them four days before they arrived at Shaw, only to find that the jungle had completely overgrown the site of my father's old village. I was to live there for ten years, until my father died. I was just a naked little native boy hidden away in the jungles of Liberia.

chapter seventeen

GIDEA'S DREAM
(1931–1932)

Though Marwieh's village had moved north without ever having come in contact with Mother Eliza, word of the mission school at Kelton had spread to many tribal villages. So it was that a constant stream of sick, hungry, troubled, and curious people visited the mission.

One morning a large group of visitors approached the clearing. Eliza saw a canopied hammock slung on the shoulders of several men, who were walking with great care. Their dress told her that they had come from beyond the Sno tribe area, and had likely walked for days. She went out and greeted them warmly.

As the men put the hammock down, she saw an emaciated old man, his skin parched and dry from fever. It was an effort for him even to open his eyes. But one look at Eliza gave him a start, as if he recognized her.

The men spoke a different dialect, but one of the boys could understand and interpret for Eliza. A hammock-bearer stepped out to speak for the weakened old man.

"My father's name is Gidea Flukah," he said, gesturing toward the shrunken man lying on the ground. "He has been sick for many months. The country doctors couldn't help him and left him to die. He knows he is old, but he has no peace. One night he had a dream—in his dream he saw a woman from across the sea. Somebody in the dream told him to find this God-woman, and she would tell him what to do. We have heard from other villages about this place, and that there was a God-woman here, so we have brought him to you."

There was no question in Mother Eliza's mind that the Holy Spirit had directed Gidea to her—she was the God-woman who had the message of life. And there was no greater joy than to tell him that Jesus loved him and had died for him.

> She was the God-woman who had the message of life.

When she had finished preaching, she got down on the ground beside the old man and took his burning hand in hers. "Old man," she began, then turned and beckoned to the interpreter, "ask him if he wants to accept Christ as His Savior."

In a barely audible voice, Gidea expressed his faith in Christ, and an expression of joy transformed him as Mother prayed for him. When Mother explained that he should come back to be baptized when he was stronger, Gidea vehemently shook his head.

Puzzled, Mother Eliza waited as he and his son discussed this for several minutes. The son turned back to Eliza, reluctantly making the proposition: "He says he must be baptized now, before he goes back home."

Though Eliza made it a policy not to baptize her converts herself, she sensed the urgency of this request. The party, now enlarged by the mission children who had gathered to listen, moved down to the creek, where Gidea Flukah was baptized in the shallow, murky waters.

He and his entourage left immediately to return home, and Mother never heard from him again. But the experience deepened her desire to spread the work of the mission into other tribal areas. Many villages only a few miles from Kelton had never heard the gospel.

After the long days in the gardens, walking to the villages, teaching, disciplining, and cooking for the children, she spent a good part of the night on her knees beside her bed praying for funds, for workers, and for the lost all around her. The girls who shared her two-room hut occasionally found her in the morning asleep on her knees, or in a chair with a Bible on her lap.

The financial burden was heavy, for her people back in Texas were hit hard by the Depression and were unable to send gifts. Father George's letters from America were discouraging.

But her own optimism, faith, and determination did not permit Mother to think of defeat. Already several of the older boys showed signs of spiritual leadership and maturity and would soon be able to start a little mission on their own. Growing in the inner recesses of her mind was the dream of taking one or two children back to be educated in the USA. Certainly Maude should have the opportunity for further training, since she had gone as far as a girl could go in Liberia.

> Her optimism, faith, and determination did not permit Mother to think of defeat.

Forces at work in the forests around her were to propel her into a decision sooner than she expected. Since the mission was fairly close to civilization, the frequent tribal wars did not usually affect life at Kelton. But in the interior the warlike Kru continued to flex their muscles.

The Kru were the last of the tribal groups to succumb to the authority of the central government in Monrovia. Spurred initially by fear of losing their valuable slave trade, they later resisted the demands of hut tax and porter services. Each side had been sniping at the other for more than a half-century.

But within the great Kru tribe were hundreds of sub-tribes. They had learned to give and take as areas became more populated and contacts with civilization caused disturbances in the delicately balanced back country ways. Land, women, power, taxes, or simple selfishness could trip the tightly wound hairspring to trigger a war.

On a lazy Sunday afternoon while "the mission children were joyfully singing in their own tongue," wrote Mother, "a messenger rushed in and gave me a letter from Rev. Birch which read as follows: 'Come to Lexington at once; the natives are fighting among themselves, and they may reach you.'"

Women were often pawns in tribal warfare. Warriors would capture women and girls, holding them for ransom or

> Women were often pawns in tribal warfare.

keeping them as wives and slaves in their own villages. With Mr. George away, the mission would be especially vulnerable to attack. The boys would most likely not be harmed as long as they were not involved in the actual fighting.

So she made a quick decision. Packing up a few belongings and leaving the older boys in charge of the mission, she took the girls and began walking back to Lexington. They would stay with the hospitable Birches for a few weeks until the fighting settled down.

But while Mother helped in the Baptist church in Lexington, working among the children and the women's missionary group, she received a letter from Father George. He pleaded with her to come back to the United States. His time there had been fraught with disappointments—a serious illness had kept him bedridden, and he had little opportunity to present the work in churches. He felt that their only hope was to go back to the National Baptist Board to see if they could help. Eliza was the logical one to do that.

With continued rumblings of war, Eliza felt that the time was right for a return to the USA. Her desire to take some children along to America now became a driving passion. Why not take two or three girls? Maude would certainly benefit from further education. Cerella was now a healthy and happy three-year-old. Mother Eliza intended to adopt her. How wonderful if she could be educated in America! Cerella could be an example to Liberian women and would be able to train other Liberian girls in Christian things.

Mother also thought of taking Fanny, who had been with her at Kelton for the past two years, but Fanny's mother would not permit it.

Mother wrote to Dr. Pleasant. She explained the conditions in Liberia and her need to return to the United States, and asked if he could raise enough for her passage.

But God was working out another plan for Eliza, one that would change the rest of her life. For two years now, Cecelia had been her adoring little shadow. She heard that Mother was taking several girls to the United States, and she longed to join them. During the weeks of waiting in Lexington, Cecelia stayed with her own mother, who worked in town. But every morning she was at the Birches, ready to run errands for Mother Eliza or to offer help wherever she could.

When Fanny's mother refused to let her go, Eliza, now obsessed with the idea of taking three girls to the States, asked Cecelia if she would like to go. Without hesitation Cecelia responded, "Oh, I'd love to go with you, Mother. Will you ask my mama?"

Cecelia's mother, who had long since relinquished any responsibility for her young daughter, voiced only one condition: "She musn't marry over there!" And it was settled.

Mother would have to apply for adoption papers for Cerella and Cecelia in Monrovia. That could take quite some time, so she decided to leave Lexington, trusting that her passage money would soon arrive. Mother and the three girls arrived in Monrovia at the end of 1931 and stayed with the Hortons for almost a year while she worked on documents and prayed for funds.

When the money came from her faithful friends in Texas, it was just enough for passage for Maude and Mother. Undaunted, Eliza reasoned that since the Lord had led her this far, and since the girls were now legally adopted, God would provide some way. So she purchased passage for herself and the three girls as far as Cadiz, Spain, where she hoped to make connections with an American-bound steamer.

To twenty-year-old Maude the sea voyage was nothing new. But Cecelia and Cerella found it a high adventure, eating the strange food in the dining room, playing with the faucets in the cabin, and sleeping on "shelves" up in the air. Mother Eliza never tired of telling the curious passengers that these little girls had just come out of the Liberian bush and were going to be trained in America.

Except for the failure of the engines for a few hours while out at sea, the trip was uneventful. But when they landed in Cadiz, they found that the steamer for the USA had left the day before. There would not be another one for months. The stranded passengers converged on the American Consul, where they were advised to travel overland to the Rock of Gibraltar in hopes of catching an Italian steamer soon to leave.

Perhaps Mother expected another miracle to stretch her funds. She and the girls left for Gibraltar, where they found the ship indeed in the harbor. But Eliza had not reckoned with reality.

"I'm sorry, Mrs. George," the clerk in the ship's office explained. "You need enough for three adult fares and one child. Even if we stretched our rules and allowed the twelve-year-old to travel half-fare, you still would not have enough money. You are short $200. There's just no way we can issue you your tickets."

chapter eighteen

MOTHER ON THE ROCK

Gibraltar evokes images of a romantic tourist haven carved out of the monumental rock guarding the mouth of the Mediterranean. But as Mother and the three girls left the shipping agent's office that December morning in 1932, the romanticism was conspicuously absent. Gibraltar looked more like the small Victorian settlement of seedy gentility that it was, crowded onto the lower edges of the Rock.

Mother and the girls would have plenty of time to investigate the fortress with its imposing guns facing seaward. But Eliza didn't know that then. With faith and self-confidence she hustled the girls to the post office to send a telegram to her sister. Jenny Belle would be able to contact her friends and supporters about the pressing financial need.

Mother understood that it might be four to six weeks before she got a response. So she decided to ask for the full $331 for passage and use the cash she had on hand for their expenses on the Rock.

Jenny vividly remembers that December morning. "I was just fixin' to drink a cup of coffee when Sister's cable asking for $331 arrived. I didn't have a penny to my name. I was so shook up I stopped drinking that coffee, and never drank another drop since."

In ensuing letters Eliza pleaded with Jenny to help "get her off the Rock." Jenny's voice still quivers when she retells the story: "I had nothing to get her off the Rock with!"

Jenny wrote daily letters contacting churches and pastors. She organized campaigns to get Mother Eliza and her girls off the Rock. Meanwhile, Eliza had to find a place to stay. The Victoria Hotel, where she and the girls had booked the first night, was not for someone of modest means.

Accommodations on the Rock were limited. Mother described the colony succinctly in her autobiography: "It has one cave, one prison house, one store, one theater building, one market, seven churches, two hotels, a reservoir, and a fort cut through the Rock.... There were only 900 inhabitants on the Rock of Gibraltar at the time I was stranded there."

Mother Eliza finally found a one-room apartment up several flights of dark, dirty stairs; it had faded Victorian wallpaper and an ancient saltwater-fed sanitation system down the hall. Gibraltar has no fresh water of its own, so its residents use water from a reservoir blasted out of the eastern side of the Rock.

God provided Mother with a Spanish landlady who was sympathetic with her plight. Sometimes she sent up tidbits from her own table. But what Cecelia remembers best about the stay on Gibraltar were Mother's prayers.

Mother prayed long prayers.

"We were praying every hour. When the clock said 'ding' we were on our knees. When we got up it was half an hour—Mother prayed long prayers. At two o'clock we were back on our knees again."

It would be six months before God chose to answer those prayers through the kind-hearted friends in the Texas Convention. Mrs. Rose Chandler Jones, who many years later would work at the new Kelton mission in Liberia, remembers the request for funds. "I must have been very young, but I can remember that every large group or convention was appealing for Mother Eliza with her little girls."

Mother began receiving checks from various friends. But as Cecelia comments, "We were thankful for the gifts, but the longer Mother stayed on the Rock the broker she got." And Mrs. Chandler Jones adds, "We would send $25 or $30, which wasn't much, and they would have to live off that. They had to live while there, and they would use up the small amounts and not have enough to go."

In spite of the hard times in those Depression years, through the kindness of churches back in Texas, Eliza finally saved enough money. Pastors like Dr. Newton Jenkins of Waco, Texas, and Dr. J. Winn of Fort Worth, helped her make her bookings on the next steamer for New York. When she walked smiling out of the agent's office in April, 1933, she had four steamship tickets and twenty-five cents in her pocket!

But Eliza's problems weren't over. In 1933 Ellis Island was still the major immigration station for the East Coast and also served as detention station for aliens and deportees. There wasn't much more that could have gone wrong as far as Eliza's documents and permits were concerned:

- she had lost her citizenship through her marriage to Mr. George;
- the two younger girls were seeking permanent residence without any visas even to enter the country;
- she did not have the $500 bond required for the two girls who weren't citizens;
- she had twenty-five cents to her name and no way to travel across the country to her destination.

A kind social worker on Ellis Island took pity on Mother and her three Liberian girls and advised her how to avoid deportation. Meanwhile, the social worker wrote to Dr. J. Winn about the funds needed to cross the country to Texas by bus, and before long the money arrived.

At the advice of the social worker, Mother wrote to a Miss Perkins, whose father was Secretary of Labor. She explained their plight and why she had brought the Liberian girls to the United States for an education.

Then there was nothing to do but wait in the virtual prison environment of the island. For five weeks Mother prayed, fasting much of that time. It was no surprise to her when the red tape and legal entanglements melted away. President Roosevelt even gave a special order releasing the girls. Mother states, "While enclosed within the walls at Ellis Island we prayed with fastings, the Lord touched hearts of the powers that be, and the door was opened, and we entered the United States without bond."

President Roosevelt gave a special order releasing the girls.

The Greyhound bus trip across the country provided the girls with a panoramic view of their new homeland. In their excitement they didn't seem to notice that the farther south they went, the more they rode in the back of the bus. Soon they were eating their lunches on their laps rather than at tables in restaurants.

But the welcome in Tyler was warm and wonderful as they were engulfed in the loving clamor and noise of a large family of aunts, uncles, and cousins. Aunt Jenny Belle took the three girls into her heart. She had no children from her brief marriage, and Cecelia and Cerella helped to fill an empty spot.

A thinner and older looking Father George was also there to greet them. Mother realized with a pang that these past three years had taken a heavy toll on him.

As Mother expected, the girls made a hit wherever they went. People loved their clipped accents and were impressed with their burden for the work in Africa. Mother soon had more offers to care for them than she could accept. It was decided that Maude would go to Eliza's alma mater, Guadalupe College, while Cerella and Cecelia would stay with Aunt Jenny Belle. Rev. S. A. Pleasant assumed the responsibility of raising funds for their education, a task he faithfully fulfilled for ten years.

But the Georges realized that they needed a promise of regular support for the work in Liberia. They had labored in Kelton on and off for the past fifteen years with no permanent buildings and no hired staff. Each time they left, the work closed down until they were able to return and start it up again.

More than ever, Eliza's heart was burdened for the villages in the interior still untouched by the gospel. How she longed to train the promising children in her care until she could send them out as missionaries themselves! She realized she could never do the job alone. But without adequate funds she had simply been eking out a hand-to-mouth existence. Though she never lost her faith and joy in the Lord, she knew there must be a better way.

As Mr. George related some of his disappointments over the past few years, Eliza realized that her people were suffering the extremes of these Depression years. They too had been in the worst of positions, not only economically, but with growing social and political frustrations as well. Black churches in America were struggling.

Ever since her call to Africa more than twenty years earlier, she had been convinced that the black churches in America should be responsible for taking the gospel to their black brothers and sisters in Africa. She had considered risking affront by approaching the more affluent white churches, but to Eliza, Liberia's salvation was a "family affair." She believed that God would eventually help her American brothers and sisters to shoulder their responsibility in Africa.

But time was running out. She was now fifty-four years old and Father George was in his mid-sixties. She had preached zealously and with deep compassion to every black church that would give her a hearing. Though many sacrificial gifts of love had been sent, no regular support had come since the split in the Convention in 1914.

Thus the Georges decided to contact white pastors in the surrounding area. The Rev. R. W. Shirley of the First Baptist Church of McAllen, Texas, invited them to come for a meeting on a Sunday evening in May 1935. Eliza joyfully recorded the result of the meeting in her autobiography.

"The summary of our messages was that God had called us to work for the salvation of our people in Africa. We also told them about the girls brought from Africa to be trained in the United States, who would return to teach their own people after they were educated. Rev. Shirley was deeply impressed. . . . It was voted immediately to pay us $30 monthly support and to give us $250 for our return passage to Africa."

The Lord also moved on the hearts of members of the Foreign Mission Board of the National Baptist Convention. The Georges attended the annual convention in Washington, D.C., in the fall of 1935 and were able to sign a contract with the Foreign Mission Board to work as regular missionaries at $30 a month. A further gift of $600 was promised for supplies and equipment. The time had come to leave for Africa.

It was difficult to say goodbye to the girls in Texas, but Mother assured them that as soon as they finished school, they would again be together. The Georges left for Liberia with the hope that this time there would be enough funds to establish a permanent work. Even the thought of having to rebuild the thatch huts at Kelton, which surely had succumbed to the elements by now, did not daunt Eliza's indomitable optimism.

chapter nineteen

FROM STEAMER TO STEAMER

(1936–1938)

And so it was back to Lexington to bide their time while preparations were made for building. Never one to sit idly, Eliza threw herself into the work of the little Baptist church in the town. It was in one of those Bible classes in early 1936 that young Henry Williamson was converted.

Mother gave Henry a part in a church program. He stumbled and stuttered so badly that his friends laughed and tittered at him. "But Mother was always encouraging," he says as he recounts the incident. "She just patted my head and told me, 'You did just fine, son.'" Henry Cicero Williamson would one day become Deputy Speaker of the Liberian House of Representatives.

Soon the first gift from the First Baptist Church of McAllen came, covering two months' salary. The women of the church sent parcels of clothing, medicine, and a sewing machine. The gifts would keep coming until the disruption of World War II.

Though the promised funds from the National Baptists did not arrive immediately, a generous donation of $300 from Dr. Pleasant and the Lincoln Association enabled the Georges and the children to move out to Kelton. For weeks they slept on the damp ground until plank floors could be laid in their mud cottages. Encouraged by the regular gifts from America, the Georges constructed larger buildings so they could accept more children.

One by one the children drifted onto the mission. Shelby Graham was brought by his father, who wanted him to learn English. He remembers Mother patting him gently and asking, "Son, can you learn?" Shelby stayed with Mother for ten years, until she sent him to high school to learn carpentry. He became Mother's "manager of oil-making," responsible for producing several gallons of palm oil for the kitchens each day, and was destined to become a respected leader in the Liberian church.

God began to send more mature, promising young people to the school. With so many children to care for and her seemingly naïve generosity, Mother seemed to live from "steamer to steamer," paying her bills and purchasing necessities when the money arrived—with long, lean periods in between.

Otto Klibo, a strong young man, volunteered to work at the mission. Father George told him that if he worked well, he would make him overseer of the boys—but Otto went further and helped to start a new mission in the interior.

Lu Mason hadn't intended to join Mother at Kelton. She had been with her some years earlier, but after Mother returned to the USA she moved back to Lexington. "I had a fall," she confesses. "I had a child."

Lu was struggling as a servant in the home of a family in town when her brother urged her to come with him to the mission. Lu refused. "I went back on Mother," she said. "I can't go to her now."

> Mother seemed to live from "steamer to steamer."

But her brother prevailed, and so, carrying a freshly baked loaf of bread as a peace offering, Lu gingerly presented herself at Mother's door. Mother was elated to see her, throwing her arms around the fearful girl. Then, holding her away from her, she chided, "Oh, Lu, you did me bad."

Lu began to sob. "I'll never do bad again if you take me back."

Eliza had an ability to forgive and encourage new beginnings. She understood the ingrained country ways that made it so difficult for young Liberians to make a clean break with the past. She also understood that Jesus taught those caught in sin, "Go and sin no more."

Lu became Mother's chief assistant, handling money for small purchases, overseeing the storeroom, and supervising the washing of the clothes. This freed Mother to do her teaching and preaching.

While Mother rejoiced in the expansion of the work, she watched with despair the deterioration of her husband. His poor health was aggravated by his drinking, which had become so severe that it could no longer be hidden from the children. Sometimes he would begin drinking early in the morning. When Mother led the children in their morning hymns he often joined in with his off-pitch melody from the bathroom.

One of the boys recalls her running down the trail shouting after Mr. George for absconding to Greenville with mission money. But most of Mother's children remember only her anguished prayers for his healing and safety.

When he was not sick or drinking, Mr. George still acted as a strict disciplinarian, lining the boys up in the morning to give them their daily tasks in the garden or on a building project. In the evening he led the singing or taught music and history to the older pupils. With so much to do on the mission, classes in those early years were usually held in the evenings around the dining tables.

Christmas of 1936 found Mother Eliza short of funds once more. Without the promised support from the Baptist Convention, all their money was soon used up on the buildings. When Father George had to make an emergency trip to Monrovia for medical care, the debts began to mount again.

But in her childlike enthusiasm, Mother wanted to make Christmas special for her children. Many of them had never celebrated Christmas before. She described the preparations in detail. "The boys cut large vines from the surrounding forests and made four swings and a merry-go-round out of cottonwood, as well as five benches. The Christmas tree was decorated with beautiful white paper in which the medicine sent by Dr. Wharton was packed. Each child received one card on the Christmas tree and two lumps of sugar. After the program that day five children were converted and baptized."

> Each child received one card on the Christmas tree and two lumps of sugar.

Early in 1937 a tribal family brought an orphaned seven-month-old girl to Eliza. The child had been left in the jungle to perish. In desperation, compassionate relatives had brought her to the mission. Though Mother had resolved not to take any more children until their financial picture improved, she could not resist this little one. She named her Leetha in honor of Rev. Shirley's wife.

God was bringing her ministry to fruition in so many ways. Rev. James Bolo and his wife had come to her some months before, pleading that she send them to the nearby village of Plahn to start a church. Rev. Bolo had been a Methodist minister for a number of years, but the denomination wanted to send him far from home, and he was not willing to go. Impressed by the devotion and experience of this man, Mother helped him become established in Plahn, some twenty miles in the interior.

In June of 1937 the first gift of $400 arrived from the Foreign Mission Board. With some of the money Mother bought cotton blankets for each child. With the remainder, she purchased supplies and sent out the Bolos as her first missionary couple.

Mother was especially burdened for the tribal children. Because their families were destitute, she never charged for tuition or food. Everything was supplied for the children through her own provision from God. Over and over they would marvel, "Everything Mother had was ours; everything we had was from Mother."

But her greatest joy continued to be the children and young people whom God was sending to the mission. One morning Mr. Joe Thomas came from Lexington with two boys who seemed to be in their late teens. Mr. Thomas introduced one boy as his nephew and the other as a country boy who had been sent to work in Lexington and placed in his care.

"Everything Mother had was ours; everything we had was from Mother."

Mr. Thomas informed Mother privately, "I want you to put more emphasis on my nephew because when I die my belongings will be for him."

But Mother didn't see things that way. She watched the two boys closely in the weeks ahead. The nephew was put to work in the kitchen, while the country boy, who had been given the Western name of Charles Carpenter, was assigned to make fences.

One day Mother called Charlie into her room to commend him for his hard work. Then she added, "Son, we are here for the natives; the town people are already civilized. Mr. Thomas said I should have special interest in his boy, but I'm telling you I'm not here for the civilized people, because they are already educated."

Then she added, "If you work hard, one day you will walk into your own house."

With that almost unfathomable incentive, Charles made a special effort to please Mother Eliza. "And," he added wryly, "that other young man cannot write his name today."

In describing how he became Mother's mission tailor, Charles also reveals the secret of her ability to stimulate her children to be more than they ever dreamed they could be. A gift of $200 had arrived from the Convention that year. In addition to the books and writing tablets Mother purchased with the money, she also bought a bolt of cloth.

One day Charles returned from a visit to Greenville, where he had dealt with a tailor about making a pair of trousers. The tailor had insulted him for being a country boy, and so he came to Mother licking his wounds.

"I paid him the money, and he just abused me," Charles told Mother.

"Son, don't you worry—you will learn how to sew. When do you plan to go to town again? Mother will pay for it."

"I can start tomorrow," Charles replied eagerly.

The next day he went to town and wandered the streets until he found a tailor he could watch at work. He stayed in Greenville for several weeks, observing the tailor's every move. When he went back to the mission, Mother asked him, "Son, where have you been?"

When he told her how he had been studying the tailor's work, Mother gave him a piece of cloth and scissors and sent him back. This time when the tailor cut, he cut, and when he got back to the mission he stitched up the trousers. What a bungle—tucks and gathers in the oddest places—too short, too wide! Charles was in despair.

When Mother came to see what he had done, he tried to hide them from her, but she pulled them out of his hands. "Son, let me see what you did." And holding them up to scrutinize them, she added, "Oh, son, you are doing well. I know you will be sewing for the mission soon."

The next time Charles went to town he looked presentable, and his second pair was much better. In a few weeks' time Mother was confident enough in his sewing that she turned the new bolt of cloth over to him, and Charles became the mission tailor.

One of the most encouraging developments on the mission that year was the hiring of a trained teacher to run the school. A Sunday school class in Texas began sending eight dollars a month for a teacher's salary, and a Mr. Nepe, educated in the USA, was hired. For the first time at Kelton there were regular school hours, with textbooks for the children.

Some of Mr. Nepe's former students followed him to Kelton. One morning Mother heard Mr. Nepe calling her to come out, saying, "Newspaper is here." Wondering how a newspaper could have been delivered when there had been no steamer for more than a month, Mother hurried outside to see a young albino man standing beside Mr. Nepe.

"Mother-Eliza, this is Newspaper, one of my former students, who would like to continue studying with me here at Kelton."

If the appearance of this pink-skinned, fair-haired African disturbed Mother, she made no sign of it. She had often wondered at the cruel combination of genes which left the albino defenseless in the merciless African sun; but the few she had met in her years in Africa had been especially bright, and Newspaper's first few words in his maturing bass voice fortified that impression.

Later, when Mother tried to get Newspaper to change his name to something more conventional, he told her, "I am the only Newspaper in the world who has life, blood, and brains." He kept the name and added George to it as he became an integral part of Mother's life.

In spite of all the changes of schedule and additional work because of her growing family, Mother never deviated from her pattern of prayer three times a day, plus Bible reading in the evenings before the children went to bed. Not knowing the language well enough to write songs in the dialect, Mother taught the children the old hymns she had grown up with. Before the breaking of the dawn, the children would wake to hear her strong voice singing "Holy, Holy, Holy." Before the girls rang the noon bell, Mother's voice would ring out "Jesus, Lover of My Soul." One of her children recalled, "Wherever one was, no matter where we were, we came."

> **Mother never deviated from her pattern of prayer three times a day.**

And it was in those times of prayer and Bible reading, kneeling around Mother as she praised and interceded, sharing with them the burdens of her heart for the heathen around them, that most of the children remember committing their lives to Christ.

And not only the children. Charles recalls that during that first year at Kelton his heathen parents came to visit him and were converted. Charles himself baptized them.

Except for Mr. George's recurring physical problems, these were the most productive and encouraging years of Eliza's experience in Africa. More than fifty children now boarded at Kelton. Young leaders were emerging who were being trained for future ministries. Though still constructed of thatch and mud, the buildings were larger and more adequate for their needs. Regular support was at last coming in, and a mission church was being planted in the interior.

But before the year was out, the first of a series of disappointments disturbed the work at Kelton. Mr. Nepe abruptly resigned over a disagreement with the Georges. The thriving school was now without a teacher.

chapter twenty

THE LIVING NEWSPAPER

The little caucus sat around Mother's table, the yellow glow from the kerosene lamp throwing a soft circle of light that just touched their faces. Mother had called in the three oldest boys after Mr. Nepe's resignation, knowing they would be deeply affected by the loss.

"Sons, I have a plan," she announced. "When I was at Guadalupe College many years ago, the principal asked me to teach some of the younger children because they didn't have enough money to hire a full staff. I think we can do the same thing here. I will teach you boys in the evenings after the younger children are in bed, and you can each teach a class in the mornings."

The quality of teaching was simple, but the children continued to learn the basics of reading and arithmetic. Meanwhile, Newspaper used every available means to quench his insatiable thirst for knowledge. When the eminent Liberian historian and politician, Richard Henries, instituted a three-month teachers' school, Newspaper was able to attend. The second year all three older boys attended the school and earned their teaching certificates.

Mother proudly proclaimed, "Now I have qualified teachers—no more need of running around to look for them."

Despite his albino myopia, Newspaper taught himself Greek, Latin, algebra, and geometry, and became an avid historian.

Many of Newspaper's students went on to high school and rose to the top of their class, even against others trained by teachers with far higher qualifications.

The school worked well under the older boys' tutelage. But toward the close of 1938 a series of events began that prompted the usually optimistic Eliza to write, "It seemed that we were being hedged in on all sides by trouble."

"We were being hedged in on all sides by trouble."

First, a shortage of water forced the children to draw their drinking water from the swamp. Though Liberia has heavy rainfall, the swampy areas are often unsuitable for drilling wells. Most people depended on streams and rivers or storage tanks. During the December–January dry season some streams dried up, causing severe problems wherever there was a concentration of people, as at Kelton.

Then a yaws epidemic broke out. Mother believed the children were exposed to the disease because tribal children with yaws had bathed in the swamp. (Medical science, however, says this virus is transmitted by direct contact with skin lesions.) Children were covered with running sores, even in their noses and under their arms. Fever and chills added to their misery.

Mother washed the sores with carbolic soap, not knowing that unless she used absolutely sterile methods she could infect other parts of the body. Under these conditions, yaws was a long, drawn-out disease, sometimes taking two years to cure. Fortunately, one attack gave lifelong immunity.

Then Cecelia wrote that she was planning on getting married later in the year. "You won't believe it," she told Mother, "but his name is Owen Davis, just like your maiden name. People will think I'm marrying my cousin. But he's a fine Christian, Mother, and wants to be a missionary. Maybe someday we'll come to Liberia together."

Mother never told Cecelia what a blow that news was to her. She had promised Cecelia's mother that she wouldn't marry in the USA.

Even during those difficult times, Mother could not resist taking in a new child. Joseph Doe, who later pastored a church in Monrovia, recalls that his sister brought him to the mission early in 1939. At first, Mother kindly but firmly refused. There had been no steamer for several months, and she didn't have blankets and clothes for the children. But seeing Joseph's fallen face, she quickly added, "Come back in a few weeks. The Lord will provide."

When Joseph started on the mission, his first job was to go to the fields where the boys were planting cassavas and keeping the flies off Father George as he sat in a chair supervising the work. Joseph quickly reassures, "Oh, he was kind, but not as kind as Mother Eliza. He didn't work, though; he just oversaw the work."

It was neither laziness nor pride that kept Father George from working. His health was fading fast, and he had little strength remaining.

One morning in January of 1939 the children could hear Father and Mother arguing. He was determined to walk to Greenville for some "supplies," but Mother tried to stop him. She could see that he was in no state for the long, hot walk, but he stubbornly refused to take her advice. "I'll be all right, Eldie. I haven't been off the mission for weeks. The change will do me good."

All that day Eliza fought a nagging fear, which was so unlike her. She continued with her daily routine—teaching, working in the garden, washing clothes—but with a sense of detachment. She tried to maintain a line of sight to the path as it broke out of the forest. When darkness fell and she could stand the suspense no longer, she sent two of the boys off toward Lexington, hoping that Father George had come that far and decided to spend the night. Eliza spent the next few hours on her knees, praying and wondering where she had failed her husband and why he had chosen the wrong path late in life.

Toward midnight she heard voices above the frog choruses in the creek. Hurrying out of the hut, she saw a procession of lanterns emerging from the bush. Leading the way was Henry Williamson and his father, from Greenville. Instinctively she knew what they had come to tell her.

The stark facts were harsh. Father had died in the home of a lady friend in Greenville, apparently of a heart attack.

In later years Speaker Williamson recalled that eerie scene. "My father took my brother and myself to her mission to announce that Father George had died. We were expecting that Mother Eliza would be frustrated. All she said was, 'Let's pray.' She led us in prayer and then got up revived and strong enough to follow us to Greenville to get the body."

In Liberia's heat, with no embalming system, it was necessary to bury the corpse within twenty-four hours. Mother and some of the children brought the body back to Kelton in a hammock that night and placed it in a simple coffin hastily constructed in a nearby village. But when she asked some of the villagers to dig a grave on the mission, they insisted on their usual payment of cane juice. With her utter distaste for liquor, Mother indignantly sent them away. Taking a few of the older boys to a sheltered spot on the edge of the mission, she took her turn with them as they dug Father's grave themselves.

What did she think as she stood the next day, surrounded by her children and friends who had come from Greenville and Lexington to pay their last respects to the man who had brought her to Sinoe? Did she ever regret her decision? Had she ever been tempted to break the contract, which had lasted twenty-one years?

Never in her letters or personal conversations did she indicate that she had made the wrong choice. When she spoke of Father George, she always remembered only the good things—his intelligence and his musical ability. She loved to recount the story of how he stood at the grave of Mrs. David Livingstone in East Africa and shed tears when he realized that this white woman had given her life to bring the gospel to his brothers and sisters in Africa. It was there that he had dedicated his life to missionary service, and that desire had brought him to Liberia.

When she spoke of Father George, she always remembered only the good things.

But few of her supporters in America remember meeting Mr. George or even hearing Mother Eliza speak of him. One of the sons of the Hortons assessed the marriage this way:

"She was very sad about that situation. I don't think [the marriage] could have worked. In the light of her character, her gifts, and her calling, it would have been difficult to find a suitable husband. She was too absorbed in working for people to give sufficient affection, attention, and time to her husband. He would have to have been exactly like her. But husbands want to take the lead and want the wife to give them a certain amount of time. It would have been hard for her unless she had changed."

When the funeral was over and her worries about Father George were laid to rest with him, Eliza collapsed. She could see no way to stay in Africa. She felt defeated, tired, and unable to cope. Even though Father George had done very little to lighten the load during recent years, she felt she could not carry on by herself.

It was in this dark hour that her investment of love in the mission children came to her rescue. One of her children recalls that after Father died, "We prayed and fasted. She had taught us to do that. We comforted her by singing 'country songs' [tribal folk songs] and civilized songs [English hymns]. We prayed fervently. Her heart 'came down,' and she started her work again."

In the years ahead Eliza would rest heavily upon the fellowship and help of her children, who had now grown into young men and women who loved God and wanted to serve Him. Many of them had watched their own parents in the villages scratch the very flicker of life out of the soil, totally dependent upon their own resources.

This was to be Kelton's fate for the next few years as the "Hitler war" touched North Africa and closed even neutral Liberia's ports to almost all traffic. Not only did this affect the finances for Mother's work, but imported goods became scarce and prices soared. Over the years Mother had become more and more Liberian in her lifestyle. Now she simply had to adapt to the country's ways.

Over the years Mother had become more and more Liberian in her lifestyle.

Meat was always limited, for the tribal people had depleted the supply of game. But hunting was one of the tribal ways to fight hunger. Mother had brought a gun with her to Liberia and knew how to shoot it, once bringing down a hawk on the wing. She taught some of the older boys how to use the weapon. They would go hunting for deer or bush cows—a dangerous African buffalo. But the most reliable source of meat was the porcupine.

Mother's attitude toward hunger and need impressed itself indelibly upon the mission children. Her faith never wavered— even when God made her wait for the answer. During this time of need the children frequently had to sit down to a meal of dry palm nuts, with its small layer of tasteless meat.

Mother instituted a practice of Monday fasts. The children all knew that this was the day Mother was not to be disturbed, but also the day when she would not punish as severely. Many times the children joined in the fasts with her, perhaps because it was preferable to another meal of palm nuts. Worse yet was the palm cabbage—the heart of the palm leaf, near the trunk, and eaten only in times of dire need.

But that's not what the children remember. They remember praying for $500 to cover a debt at the Dutch store in Greenville. They prayed and fasted for several days, singing a ditty to the tune of "Glory, Glory, Hallelujah." "Five hundred dollars is a wise word . . . to glorify our Lord."

When at last a ship came to Greenville in 1939 and blew its horn, it was heard miles away on the mission. Mother and several boys hurried to the beach in great anticipation. Charles reports, "She came back saying, 'Oh children, the money is here.' And so it was. Now she could pay her bills. But there was still nothing for us to live on."

She determined not to give in to discouragement, even when she was down to one dress to wear.

Whether it was making soap from the edoe root's ashes, or salt by boiling off seawater from the drums the boys lugged from the beach, Mother looked at every challenge as an exciting adventure and a team effort. She determined not to give in to discouragement, even when she was down to one dress to wear. When it was time to wash it, she warned the children not to come in while she dried it over the fire. The rest of her wardrobe had long since been remade into clothes for the children or given to tribal women in exchange for produce.

The villagers often took advantage of Mother's love and concern. They borrowed money and asked favors, knowing she found it hard to turn them down. When the steamship whistle blew in Sinoe's port, the locals knew Mother might be getting money. Before she or her boys were back from Greenville, they were arriving on the station carrying cassavas, plantains, peanuts, and other produce to sell. Eliza often instructed her children to buy something from each person. She wanted each one to go away with a little money, if only one or two cents.

The sheer grit of the times was summarized in a banner she had the boys hang over the entrance to the dining room: LIFT-ING OTHERS AS WE CLIMB.

Through all the turmoil, Mother realized that the fulfillment of her dream to send out young missionaries was drawing closer. Newspaper had recently been ordained by the Liberian Baptist Association and was preaching regularly in nearby villages. Charles and Petro were also preaching, with the hopes of being ordained soon.

She had taught them all she could, and they were ready to move on. She also sensed that strong attractions between the older boys and certain girls could no longer be denied. Marriage had been deferred much longer here at the mission than back in the villages, where girls were given to their husbands soon after puberty.

Lu Carpenter says that Mother was concerned when she noticed that "boys and girls started loving. She said to me, 'You be good now, and don't do bad again.'"

When Lu showed an interest in one of the boys on the mission, Mother advised, "No, don't look to that boy. You must look again. You are civilized; you must make something of yourself. Don't think that boy will go far. There are other boys here."

When Lu and Charles began to pay special attention to each other, Mother approved but with this warning, "All right, but if you are grown-up enough to love, you ought to get married."

The surrounding villages were now begging for missionaries to start a church and a school. But before Mother could help the young couples get married and then send them out, she needed more money.

Even the building situation on the mission was critical. Termites had undermined the foundations of the main mission house, and part of it had fallen in. Once again she fell back on her only Source of supply. This time she divided the children into "prayer committees," giving each little group one item to pray for:

lumber for a substantial mission house
zinc for roofs for buildings
a large canoe to go to Sinoe and upstream villages
Bibles and songbooks
more girls to attend the school
new friends for the mission
funds for the work at large, including new missions
safe return of girls from America.

In 1940 only $180 came in to supplement the regular support from the McAllen Baptist Church. But after Mother implemented the prayer committees, almost $1500 was received in 1942.

The main mission house was rebuilt that year, and Newspaper and Francis were married and sent to the town of Seedor, some eight miles away. The town leaders had erected a church building and were urging Mother Eliza to send a pastor. Her first missionary couple had been launched!

chapter twenty-one

DOH GETS A NEW NAME

*L*ife was very hard for our family in the interior. Even though the tribal war was over, soldiers would still come to our village and demand that we give them our chickens or goats and other things. We couldn't afford to lose our meager supplies, but we were afraid to resist.

Though we were very poor, my mother always found ways to take care of strangers when they passed through our village. Her own mother, Dehwlo, had been known as the "Kleba Nyonnoh," or the most generous person in the village, and my mother, Nyonobe, tried to follow her example as best she could.

But I resented it whenever strangers passing through the village were invited to our house. At first Mother allowed me and my two brothers to eat with the guests, but I made a pig of myself, stuffing my mouth with handfuls of rice and grabbing another handful before I could swallow even what I had. Mother was ashamed of me. She wouldn't let me eat with the guests after that. Then I would just sit and glare at the visitors, making them feel uncomfortable until they would invite me to the table. From then on Mother made me sit outside the house until the guests had finished eating.

I don't know what made me so incorrigible. In fact, the whole village asked that question. "What's the matter with that son of the Marwiehs?" they would ask. My poor parents were at their wits' end.

Even though I loved my mother dearly, I found myself doing terrible things. I can remember seeing her sitting on a bench outside the house and impulsively picking up a stick to throw at her legs. I missed her and struck a child, hurting him badly.

At times like that the villagers would join my parents in meting out a punishment. That time they held me down on the ground by my legs and arms while they poured a bowl of hot pepper soup down my nose. I nearly choked to death, and for hours afterward my nose burned.

I couldn't understand myself. After one of those episodes I would go off into the forest and pound my head against a tree, crying, "What's wrong with me? I should kill myself." I hated being the "white sheep" of the family.

But one day when I was about twelve years old, a boy returned to our village from the coast, where he had been visiting his father. None of us younger ones had ever seen the ocean, so we crowded around him to hear all about it. It was as though he had been to the moon and back.

Enjoying the acclaim, he kept us spellbound with his experiences as he recounted the strange things he saw. Among other things, he told us about how some people on the coast met together in a house on Sundays, and there they sang and stayed a long time. He couldn't figure out what they were doing, and finally his curiosity got the better of him, so he asked one of the villagers, "What do you do in there for such a long time?" They told him they were praying to God who created everything, and they said they believed He heard their prayers.

I had never heard anything like this, but it excited me, and I wanted to pray to God too. I asked the boy to meet me on Sunday, and we would go someplace outside the village and he could tell me how to pray. But he wasn't interested.

Disappointed, I decided the next Sunday to try it by myself. I went to a hut that my cousin was still building, and with no one around I tried to pray for the first time. I had never heard anyone pray before, but I decided I would just talk to this God as if He were my father. I can't explain what happened, but it was an exciting experience — I wanted to know more about this God, but there was no one in our village who knew anything about Him. So for two years I kept praying by myself and hoping that someday someone would come along who could tell me more.

About this time the government started building a motor road to prepare for automobiles, and I (along with most of my male relatives) spent two weeks per month for the next two years building roads, under terrible working conditions.

Then I went back to Seedor, where I had been born, and stayed with my cousin. There I made the most wonderful discovery of my life, for in Seedor there was a church house, and people met together, to pray to the God who created the world.

How excited I was! I could hardly wait for Sunday to come. All night I lay on my mat, waiting for the bell that my cousin said would ring to call people to church.

That morning I sat at the back of the church, listening to a preacher tell me about God for the first time in my life. I found that He was far more wonderful than I had ever imagined back in Shaw. The preacher said that God loved the world so much that He sent His only Son, Jesus, to take away my sins. I wondered if He knew how terrible I was and the awful things I had done back in my village. But the preacher said that no matter what I had done, God would forgive me and make my heart clean again.

I knew it was all true; hadn't this God heard my prayers back in Shaw when I talked to Him and asked Him to help me? Hadn't He sent me here to Seedor when I didn't even know He had one of His churches here?

I gave my heart to God that morning; it was nice to know He had a Son too — He was really a Father, just like I had been praying to Him.

The first thing I wanted to do after that was to go back home and tell my mother, Nyonobe. She would be so glad to know that her white sheep was a different person. And I wanted her to know that God loved her too.

Before I could go home, another wonderful thing happened to me. The preacher told me he had a school in the village, and that if I could get something to wear — he didn't allow naked children — I could come to his school.

I rushed home to tell my cousin all these good things, but he discouraged me. "You have nothing to wear, Doh, and I have only what I have on, so I can't give you anything."

But then my cousin's wife interrupted him. "Tar, he can wear my booba (blouse). I wear it only when I'm going visiting. He can bring it back to me every day after school if I need it."

Tar scoffed at that. "Whoever heard of a boy going to school in a booba? I'm sure Teacher Newspaper wouldn't allow it."

But so determined was I to go to school that I didn't mind what I wore, and I dashed over to the church house where Teacher Newspaper and his wife lived, to ask him if I could come to school in a booba.

"It doesn't matter what you wear, Doh. I'll try to get a shirt from Mother Eliza for you as soon as I can, but for now the booba is just fine." Then he added, "And since you're going to be learning and getting civilized, I think you need a new name — a civilized name. I'll think about that too."

The next morning I appeared at the church house long before the bell for school rang, dressed in my cousin's white blouse, which hung to my knees. And when Newspaper introduced me to the other children in the class, I found that he had decided on my "civilized name" — from now on I was to be Augustus Marwieh.

Augustus would soon become a mainstay in Mother Eliza's ministry. Newspaper and his wife had been at Seedor for just over a year when Mother sent an urgent message that they return to Kelton. Another teacher had left, and with now over 100 children on the mission, she could not manage without Newspaper's help. And so Newspaper and his wife and three of the students living with them—Morris Campbell, Andrew Saydee, and Augustus Marwieh—returned to Kelton.

Mother welcomed the boys warmly. She was excited to learn that Morris was already a gifted preacher and a brilliant student as he studied under Newspaper and soaked up all the knowledge he could. Morris had a spiritual maturity and zeal for God that touched a respondent chord in Mother's heart, and she sensed that he had leadership potential she could put to use.

On the other hand, Augustus was small for his fifteen years. His voluminous eyes seemed as oversized for his face as did the khaki hand-me-down shirt draped over his thin body. He gave Mother a shy smile when he was introduced to her. He had heard so much about this "God-woman" that he was tongue-tied, though he managed to stammer a Kru "thank you" for the shirt she had sent out of the mission barrel—the first piece of clothing he had ever owned.

Newspaper hastened to assure Mother that his unlikely protégé was a good student and would learn English quickly. In the months ahead Mother

Mother nicknamed Augustus "local preacher."

nicknamed Augustus "local preacher," for this once-tongue-tied youngster was soon preaching with the best of them.

It's not that Mother had much extra time for the new students that Newspaper had brought—she was busy preparing for Charles and Lu's wedding.

Mother did not necessarily disapprove of the traditional dowry system of marriage practiced by the tribal people. But when her own children on the mission married, she gave them a typical Western wedding with all the trappings. Charles and Lu were given royal treatment—a white dress for Lu, flowers, a huge meal for all the guests on the station, and a wedding journey to Wedjah, forty miles inland from the coast.

For some time now Mother had been receiving requests from the chief of the Juarzon District to start a school. Only one other elementary school existed in the whole district, and thousands of tribal children had never had the opportunity to attend school. Mother had been praying about the needs in that area for quite awhile. Now, with the marriage of the Carpenters, the day had arrived when she could send a missionary couple to start a work for God in Juarzon.

Since the Sinoe River was navigable for only a few miles inland, the newlyweds traveled by foot on narrow jungle trails. Several of the younger children accompanied them, carrying the few household items that Mother had been able to accumulate for them. But no honeymoon couple ever left with more anticipation or good wishes than the Carpenters as they set off on their long trek that July afternoon in 1943.

But in the midst of the fulfillment of Mother Eliza's dreams, tragedy struck. Leetha was a precocious child who had made a commitment to Christ when she was only five years old. In a sense, she had filled the void created by Cerella's departure.

It started with a simple throat infection. Mother tried her home remedies, but the hot little body continued to burn with fever. With no doctor within 200 miles, Mother felt helpless as she watched the suffering child tossing and turning on the bed. She sat up with Leetha night after night, bathing and soothing her, listening to her delirious prattle, trying to get her to take a few sips of water to cool her parched lips.

Toward daylight after one particularly difficult night, Leetha seemed to come out of her delirium. She nestled into Mother's arms as she whispered her last prayer into her ear: "Lord, bless Mother Eliza, all the mission children, and me, for Jesus' sake. Amen."

Instead of sending another little girl to the mission, as she had prayed, God took Leetha home. She was buried on the mission beside Father George that day.

When her family in the tribe heard of Leetha's death, the leaders came to demand reparations of $250—a Sno-country custom if a tribal member dies in an area outside his home. They believed that an evil curse had fallen upon Leetha, and that she had succumbed because she was outside her own tribal protections.

Wearily, Mother allowed the older mission boys to settle the matter with the men, knowing that they understood the customs. The chief and his men reluctantly agreed not to press charges and left the mission without disturbing Mother again.

But even this sorrow could not dampen Mother's joy in at last expanding her work into the interior. By the end of 1943 there were four substations in addition to Kelton under Mother's supervision. Early in 1944 the pastors and leaders of the churches in these areas gathered to form the "Pleasanton Baptist Association," named in honor of the beloved Texas pastor who had so faithfully backed Mother's work. Rev. James Bolo was elected the first moderator of the association. Rev. Newspaper George became the secretary, and Rev. Charles Carpenter was the treasurer.

At sixty-five years of age Mother Eliza's lifelong dreams were coming to fruition. Now if only the girls she had sent to the USA for training would return to help her, she was sure she could open more schools and churches in the interior, where so few had ever heard the gospel.

chapter twenty-two

THE GIRLS RETURN

When the letter arrived from the National Baptist Convention, Mother felt as if the clock had been turned back thirty years to the time when another letter from another board changed the course of her life.

She had been corresponding with Maude and Cerella, urging them to come back to Africa. Maude had completed her B.S. degree in Florida and had also finished a practical nurses' course at Baylor University Hospital in Texas. Cerella had wrapped up a high school course in secretarial work. Neither girl was clear about her plans.

But now the letter from the Foreign Mission Board finalized everything. Dr. J. P. Reeder, the corresponding secretary of the National Baptist Convention, and Mrs. M. A. B. Fuller, the president of the Women's Missionary Union, were bringing the girls back to Africa. The Baptist officials were looking forward to seeing the work they had been supporting for so many years.

Busy days of preparations followed. Newspaper, who had joined Morris in the work at Butaw, was recalled to help plan the occasion. Mother was adept at giving a Liberian welcome. She gathered the workers and other church leaders from the submissions, and prepared a lengthy program of speeches and choir numbers.

Few of the children she now had would remember Maude and Cerella. It had been thirteen years since the girls had left

chapter twenty-two

THE GIRLS RETURN

When the letter arrived from the National Baptist Convention, Mother felt as if the clock had been turned back thirty years to the time when another letter from another board changed the course of her life.

She had been corresponding with Maude and Cerella, urging them to come back to Africa. Maude had completed her B.S. degree in Florida and had also finished a practical nurses' course at Baylor University Hospital in Texas. Cerella had wrapped up a high school course in secretarial work. Neither girl was clear about her plans.

But now the letter from the Foreign Mission Board finalized everything. Dr. J. P. Reeder, the corresponding secretary of the National Baptist Convention, and Mrs. M. A. B. Fuller, the president of the Women's Missionary Union, were bringing the girls back to Africa. The Baptist officials were looking forward to seeing the work they had been supporting for so many years.

Busy days of preparations followed. Newspaper, who had joined Morris in the work at Butaw, was recalled to help plan the occasion. Mother was adept at giving a Liberian welcome. She gathered the workers and other church leaders from the submissions, and prepared a lengthy program of speeches and choir numbers.

Few of the children she now had would remember Maude and Cerella. It had been thirteen years since the girls had left

156

Liberia. But the children had heard Mother praying for the two so many times that they seemed like part of the family.

The reunion in Greenville was a time of laughing and crying, all talking at once, remembering their last trip together. Names of family and friends spilled over the conversation. How's Mama? Is Jimmy still there? How about the Birches and the Hortons?

> The reunion in Greenville was a time of laughing and crying.

But Mother couldn't neglect Dr. Reeder and Mrs. Fuller, who on their first trip to this steamy land were looking uncomfortable and a bit apprehensive. Eliza arranged for the guests to be taken partway to the mission by canoe. By now the mission house had been rebuilt, and the children were crowded together in the other huts so the guests could have rooms on the second floor. How the children had scoured the plank floor and pounded and scrubbed Mother's few sheets at the river "laundry" until they were almost as white as new!

Mother planned for Maude and Cerella to stay with her for the time being, and then make other arrangements after the board members had gone.

The children and church workers waited at the mission most of the day in excited anticipation. Posting lookouts on the trail, they spent the day singing and talking endlessly. Mother marveled at how the tribal people never seemed to run out of things to discuss. And of course the workers who had come from their scattered posts clustered together, comparing their problems and successes.

Village women arrived to help prepare the festive meal. They gathered in the outdoor kitchens, stoking their open fires under the simmering kettles, lifting the lids to check the progress.

Children scampered in and out of the crowds, playing tag, teasing and taunting each other. Babies were jostled on big sisters' backs until they began to howl, then were quickly transferred to their mothers, liberating the babysitters to scamper away and join the fun.

Knowing that Mother disapproved of nakedness, the village women wore colorful cloth over their breasts. Their bright, hand-woven lappas (wraparound skirts) were matched with imaginatively tied head scarves.

When at last the party was spotted down the trail, the crowd surged forward, singing and clapping, performing little dance steps of welcome. The happy group accompanied the tired travelers into the thatched church.

Each of Mother's children gave a speech.

One after another, each of Mother's children gave a speech, thanking the visitors for their help over the years and warmly welcoming the two girls. Deacons and women's leaders from the sub-stations spoke in their native dialects; Newspaper acted as interpreter and master of ceremonies. A dozen choirs shared in the program, their drums beating a persistent accompaniment, syncopated clapping accenting the African rhythm.

The female guests were presented with colorfully woven "lappas," the traditional women's dress. Dr. Reeder was bedecked in a handwoven chief's robe. Already sweltering in his dark suit and tie, it must have taken an effort for Dr. Reeder to thank the donors. He couldn't have known the tremendous sacrifice this gift represented!

When the excitement died down, and the people returned to their homes, Mother and Dr. Reeder, Mrs. Fuller, and Maude began their discussions. It was not clear to Mother what they had in mind.

Mrs. Fuller was insistent that Mother return home for a rest. "You've been here for ten years, Mother, without a vacation of any kind. Maude and Cerella are here now to help you, and this is a good time for you to come back."

Mother had hoped to stay and help Maude get started on the work. Cerella was to assume the secretarial duties and teach some of the girls to type and keep simple books. Mother finally conceded that it might be better to take a break first, and let the girls maintain the station.

But Dr. Reeder's second suggestion met with Mother's adamant refusal. They felt the mission was too difficult to reach—off the road, far from town. "We would like to move the work to Monrovia where it will be closer to the center of activity and easier to maintain communications," said Dr. Reeder.

Mother was aghast! There were dozens of churches in Monrovia. And what about the native children, who were not yet welcome in civilized society? Where would they go to school? Who would spread the gospel to the tribes in the hinterland, who had never once had a missionary come and tell them about Christ?

"Why haven't you come before to tell us about Him?"

"Why, Dr. Reeder, when I visit some of those tribes and tell them that Jesus died for them, they ask me, 'Why haven't you come before to tell us about Him?'"

Desperate, Mother sent word for Newspaper to come back to the station to help defend her position. After days of discussions, Dr. Reeder finally agreed that, rather than going to Monrovia, they would move the mission a few miles south to the new motor road. The first automobile had already been introduced into Sinoe County.

Concerned for the future of her beloved substations, which were far more isolated than Kelton, Mother urged Dr. Reeder and Mrs. Fuller to visit one. The most accessible was in Butaw, where Newspaper had gone several months earlier to help Morris

Campbell. The work in Butaw had grown so fast that Mother felt it warranted another missionary, so Augustus Marwieh had joined his teacher.

Gus says today, "I well remember the frantic preparations that we made on the station and how we practiced saying, 'How do you do, Dr. Reeder?'"

Before the officials of the Foreign Mission Board left Liberia, they acquired a 1000-acre site along the motor road for the "new Kelton," which would now be named after the National Baptist Convention. They also acquired deeds to the property of the thatch-and-mud edifice of the Morning Star Baptist Church in Butaw.

Mother bid her tearful and fearful good-byes to Maude and Cerella and the rest of her children, and began her unwilling journey home. A day out to sea from Monrovia, Dr. Reeder finally revealed everything to a shocked and heartbroken Mother Eliza.

"Mother, you have done a heroic and commendable work in Liberia, but we have felt for some time that you were getting too old to continue directing the mission. When Maude offered her services as a missionary in Liberia, she came with fine credentials. You can be very proud of that young lady, coming from the background she has, and today she has a bachelor's degree.

"Mother, we have decided to retire you."

"But Maude felt that it would be very difficult to work under you, especially since she has been well-educated and has new ideas. She was also concerned about you. You have labored in Africa for thirty-two years, under very difficult conditions. You've had malaria over and over; the ulcers on your legs from walking in those swamps never seem to heal. Surely God is satisfied with your long years of service too.

"Therefore, Mother, we have decided to retire you. You can continue going around to churches to raise support for the work, and we will send it out to Maude. But we will not agree to sending you back to Kelton again."

Mother sat in stunned silence. She ventured one burning question: "Will you also be responsible for my substations?"

Dr. Reeder had some very strong opinions on this too, but he tried to be gentle. "Well, Mother, we feel you may have extended yourself too far. The work at Kelton needed every bit of money and attention you could give it. Instead, you have sent your best leaders out into the interior, thus also taking financial support from the school. We feel you should have concentrated on developing a strong school, and that's what we're going to do."

Mother felt as if she had been slapped in the face.

"However," he added hastily, "since we have registered the Butaw work in the name of the National Baptist Convention, we will continue to support the work of Brother George there."

God gave Mother the grace to say quietly, "All right, Dr. Reeder. I'll retire."

In her autobiography Mother reported the action of the board simply: "In 1945 the Foreign Mission Board of the National Baptist Convention of America saw fit to discontinue my services as a missionary."

Though Mother acquiesced to her forced retirement, inwardly she was not at all sure this was God's direction. She reminded herself, "The Convention didn't call me; God Almighty called me."

For a time she rested at home with her sisters Jenny Belle and Ellen. Papa had died years earlier, and the little house in Tyler seemed strangely empty.

> "The Convention didn't call me; God Almighty called me."

Mother waited anxiously for word from Africa. When News-paper's first letter arrived, her fears were confirmed. The Convention had written him that they had retired Mother Eliza, and they would no longer be supporting the sub-missions. If the workers wished to receive a stipend, they would have to return to work at Kelton. Morris Campbell had already joined forces with Maude, but the other children were determined to man their stations as long as they could.

Now that the mission had retired her against her wishes, these friends came to her aid.

That was all Mother Eliza needed to seal her decision—she would return to Africa to work by faith. After all, isn't that what she had been doing the thirty-two years she was there?

Her sacrificial life and sweet spirit had won her many friends. Now that the mission had retired her against her wishes, these friends came to her aid.

Mother began a diligent letter campaign. Before long she had booked a heavy schedule of meetings, taking her through Texas and into California, where some of the Baptist churches had begun to take an interest in her work. One of her friends from Texas, Mrs. Elle Mae Gibbs, had moved to Oakland, and invited Mother to use her home for as long as she stayed. Through Elle Mae's eyes the Mother Eliza of deputation times emerges.

"I invited her to come and stay with me," Elle Mae recalls. "Every time she came back to California she would stay in my home. At that time the Baptists had put her down; they were not going to support her anymore. I believe the men in the denomination didn't want to send her. They didn't think a woman was capable of staying there under the conditions she had to live under.

"I suppose Mother didn't want to relinquish her authority over what she had built up over the years, and you couldn't blame her for that."

Mother Eliza, with her sparkling sense of humor, proved to be a delightful houseguest. She had the ability to keep herself entertained without making demands on her hostess. Her prayer life, too, was a constant source of wonder to the people with whom she stayed.

"I had a two-bedroom house," Elle Mae remembers. "The bedrooms were across the hall from each other. I remember waking up in the middle of the night hearing Mother Eliza praying. Sometimes it would go on for an hour or more. I would drop off to sleep and wake up, and she would still be praying. The next morning she would ask, 'Honey, did I disturb you last night?' She would sometimes pray almost all night, so burdened was she for the work in Africa and the people she had left behind."

She would sometimes pray almost all night.

One day while Mother was staying at her house, Elle Mae asked, "How would you like me to organize a club to help support you?"

That was the beginning of several Eliza Davis George clubs. For the next ten years, the clubs sent gifts of food and clothing to the mission.

Mrs. Channel belonged to a club of about fifteen women in Oakland. She sorrowfully commented, "So many of our people are not interested in foreign missions. They think we have enough to do at home—that Africa is such a wealthy continent."

But with the backing of the California club and an active group of women in Houston, plus several faithful churches, Mother felt confident that she had a sufficient support base to return to Africa. She persuaded Cecelia to go back to help with the work. Cecelia had been longing to return to Africa for some time. Her own mother was ill, and she wanted to see her again.

Though Cecelia's husband also felt called to Africa as a missionary he did not yet have any Bible training. Nor did he feel it was wise to go out under Mother's supervision when she was not connected with any official organization. The National Baptist Convention agreed to send him, but only after he had taken several years of additional training. So in 1946 Cecelia and her three children left for Liberia with the understanding that when he had completed his training he would join them.

Cecelia shared Mother's burden for her lost people, and she felt obligated to return to Liberia, knowing that Mother had brought her to the USA to be trained to go back to Africa. So, though it was difficult to leave her husband and face the uncertainties of life in the interior with little children, far from medical care or easy communications, this was the lesser of two evils.

Cecelia recalls that Liberia was a new world—far different from her memories as a child. In fourteen years of life in the West she had forgotten that there were no conveniences in the bush. Stationed at first in Butaw, where Newspaper George and his wife had a little school, Cecelia recounts: "We were ten miles from Greenville and the nearest stores. I had to get used to using kerosene or palm-oil lamps, cutting wood for cooking, and carrying buckets of water."

Later they moved even further inland, to Plahn, taking the boarding children with them and opening a school in the village where the elderly James Bolo pastored a church. Now they were twenty-five miles from the coast. Cecelia remembers "walking everywhere, carrying loads on my head."

In Plahn they were given a plot of ground to start a school. They built a hut "like everyone else's, dirt floor and all." Cecelia quickly relearned how to plant a Liberian farm—rice, cassavas, a pepper patch, and vegetables—for there was little money coming from Mother Eliza.

During the rainy season, when they could not live off the garden, "There were times when we didn't have anything. We would use the last little pint of rice for breakfast, asking the Lord to send us something for dinner. And He always did. Someone would come by to see his or her child and bring a little rice. The parents appreciated so much what we were doing, for there was no other school at all in the district.

"We didn't have Bibles or books. We just used old magazines to train the children to read. I had to use an interpreter, but Newspaper carried on the ministerial part. He was a good minister."

Cecelia had left her three children with Sister Maude at new Kelton when they moved the mission to the Plahn area. From time to time she would make the long trek back through the jungle to visit them.

On one such visit in 1947 Cecelia strangely felt that she should have brought her black dress. Nearing the turnoff to Butaw, she met a man who recognized her and gave her a letter he had been instructed to carry to Plahn. Opening the letter, her odd premonition began to take shape—Maude was very ill in the government hospital in Greenville.

The accounts of Maude's final illness are not clear. Some say she was poisoned; Cecelia says she had a burst appendix. But she also describes her symptoms: "She couldn't drink because when we carried a cup to her mouth, her jaw would lock."

Maude had been in Africa barely two years when she died. Cecelia and Cerella held her in their arms while the terrified nurse fled from the room.

After Maude's death Cerella married one of the men from Greenville. She was no longer interested in carrying on Mother's work, and she started to work at the first branch bank. Within three years Cecelia returned to the USA with her ailing husband, who could not withstand Liberia's fever-inducing illnesses.

Years later, in 1952, Mrs. Rose Chandler Jones, who helped found one of Mother Eliza's "clubs," went with her husband to serve at the new Kelton. Her report of what she found is ironic:

> There was nothing there. Rev. Davis, Cecelia's husband, had already taken sick and left, and the mission house was used for a way station. Passersby would go in and warm up, building a fire in the middle of the plank floor. They scorched the floors, and, well, they just ran the place down. It had been empty for a year because Mr. Davis got malaria.
>
> The place was in debt. Maude had taken a lot of money to appease the people, but she just couldn't run the mission. When we got there, it was in a rundown condition with nothing going on. There wasn't even a church.

None of the three girls on whom Mother had pinned her hopes had been able to fulfill her dreams. She would have to look elsewhere for someone to carry on her work.

chapter twenty-three

BIG PLANS
(1948–1949)

*M*other Eliza's appearance in Plahn on a rainy day in October 1948 seemed like a mirage to Newspaper and Cecelia. Mother did not depend on the haphazard communication system of the country. She preferred to arrive unannounced.

The Horton brothers often saw Mother Eliza coming down the road toward their house in Monrovia, having just gotten off the ship. "We thought she had retired several times, but there she was again," they remember. "In later years she would appear in a taxi, and Mama Horton would yell out, 'There's Mother Eliza!' We would all run out and kiss her and welcome her. In the evening, after supper, she would braid Mama's hair, and we would all sit around listening to her experiences."

This time when she stopped at the Hortons' on her way through Monrovia she told them how she almost didn't make it back to Liberia. "Why, dearie [her name for Ora], I went to the shipping company in New Orleans to book my passage, and would you believe it, they told me I was too old to travel by ship! Why, I'm only sixty-nine, I told them, but they wouldn't sell me a ticket."

Reaching over to get another candy out of the dish Ora had placed within easy reach, knowing her weakness for sweets, Mother went on: "I thought to myself, *That won't stop me.* I went to the airport and asked how old a person had to be to fly. They told me there's no age limit. 'As long as you've got the money, you fly.' So I got on that plane and came right to Africa where I'm supposed to be, because I'm determined that my bones will bleach on African soil."

But now, back in the interior village of Plahn after a twenty-mile hike through the jungle, Mother must have surveyed her new mission with frustration. After all the years of hard work and persistent pioneering at Kelton, she was starting all over again.

The school that Newspaper and Cecelia had started was meeting in a brush arbor, the sapling framework covered with a thatch of palm leaves. *Hardly durable enough to last through the rainy season*, thought Mother.

"I'm determined that my bones will bleach on African soil."

A little two-room, mud-and-thatch hut served as a home for the Georges and Cecelia and the few boarding children. Mother was glad to see that Augustus was still with Newspaper, and was now a bright-eyed young man who, according to Newspaper, was a brilliant student.

Otto Klebo came by to welcome her too. He was living in his home village of Plandibalibo, about ten miles away, where he had also started a church. The workers proudly told Mother that the two little missions were part of an association called the Elizabeth Native Interior Mission (ENI), which also included the sub-mission at Wedjah.

Mother could not keep back the tears as she surveyed her faithful children—Otto, Petro, Newspaper, James Bolo, Cecelia, Phillip Sota, and Charles and Lu at Wedjah. All of them would still be primitive, unevangelized country people if God had not brought her to train them and teach them about Him. Only Cecelia had gained the privilege of advanced training. Perhaps if God permitted her another ten years, other native children could be trained as pastors and teachers. Somewhere there was one who could take her place.

At their first discussion regarding the future of the work, Mother announced to the workers that she would take a boy to America the next time she went back. "No more girls," she stated firmly. She wanted to take Andrew Saydee, one of the promising students at Kelton, but the others disagreed. They were unanimous that Augustus Marwieh was the better student and would more likely make a good leader.

Mother agreed to observe him closely while she was at Plahn. If he were indeed all they said he was, she would take him back with her the following year. For the moment she suggested that they not tell him about the plan.

One day Mother asked Augustus to accompany her to a nearby village to hold a service. As they were walking back to the mission, Mother decided the time had come to broach the subject.

"Gustus, perhaps you know that I've been thinking about taking a boy to America to get trained so he can come back to serve his people."

> Gus had been dreaming and praying about this moment for more than four years.

Gus's heart jumped to his throat. He had heard some talk that Mother wanted to take Andrew, but his own heart had told him that would not be so.

"So, Gustus, the others recommended that I take you. They said you were clever and would make a fine leader. I've been watching and praying, son, and I believe the time has come for you to make plans to go to America with me."

Make plans! Gus had been dreaming and praying about this moment for more than four years. He had, in his own words, "absolute confidence that God would let me go to America."

Everywhere he had gone, whether to Butaw, Kelton, and now Plahn, he had found a "praying ground" to remind God of such promises as "ask and you will receive." He had prayed that he would be allowed to go to study in America. But no one—not even Mother Eliza or Newspaper—knew what he had been praying about.

When asked in later years how a native boy from the hinterland of Liberia would develop such an ambition, he could only respond, "from God." His was not a dream of wealth or power or even prestige, but a God-given desire to study so that he could serve among his own people.

Gus couldn't articulate these longings to Mother on that day in late 1948, but it was as if she could read his heart. The same divine spark that had sent him to the "praying ground" now drove her to do everything she could to get him overseas.

For six months Mother trudged from the offices of the American consulate to the post office to the Liberian government offices, speaking to every official of influence in Monrovia, seeking permission for Gus to go to the United States with her.

Although he was twenty years old, Gus had completed only the fifth grade. The USA would issue student visas only to high-school graduates. Mother tried to obtain an immigrant's visa for him, but failed in that as well, and finally had to concede that she could not take him to the USA this time. Leaving him in the loving and capable care of the Horton family while he attended school, Mother returned once again to America to raise more funds for her struggling ENI mission.

When she returned a year later, the picture couldn't have been much bleaker. The little thatch schoolhouse at Plahn had burned down. Most of the children had gone back home, and Newspaper had left the work. At seventy-one years of age there was nowhere to go but up.

chapter twenty-four

THE "CURSED" PLACE
(1950)

Otto chopped the overhanging vine blocking their way so that Mother could follow him through the thick underbrush. They had left the narrow path several miles back and were now in totally uninhabited territory, though it was only five or six miles from Otto's home village of Plandibalibo.

When the villagers heard where Otto was taking Mother, they had urged her not to go. "Mother, you shouldn't pass that way—that's the devil bush. One man went there and tried to make a farm, and after three days he just died, and nobody knows how he died. Mother Eliza, you shouldn't go."

But Mother simply reassured them, "We'll be all right, children. Don't worry, God will protect us."

As she and Otto walked away into the forest she could hear them muttering about her "strong medicine."

"They don't know that my strong medicine is the Lord, do they, Otto? Maybe someday they will learn to trust Him rather than the ju-jus they hang above their houses to protect them."

Mother and Otto walked in silence for several minutes. Only the swish of Otto's cutlass (a tool similar to a machete) as he cleared a path and the buzz of the flies around their heads broke the hot silence.

As she walked Mother prayed, "Lord, let this be the right place. You know I don't have much more time to build a lasting work for you."

After consulting with the other workers, Mother decided to leave Plahn even though she had already rebuilt the thatch schoolhouse. The government had begun to place teachers in interior villages, but they sent J. D. Sahnyenneh to Plahn. When Sahnyenneh complained that the children chose to go to Mother's school rather than his, she determined to move on.

"Liberia is too big and schools are too few for us to quarrel about the children in this village," she said. "I'll just go further into the interior where there are no schools."

And so this morning in 1950 Otto was leading her to a "cursed place." As they neared the spot, the ground began to rise slightly. When Otto said, "This is it," they were standing on the heavily forested crest of a small knoll, with virgin jungle stretching out before them, a murky creek pulsing over submerged logs along the bottom of the hill.

Otto asked once more, "Mother, are you sure you want to build a mission on this land?"

"Son, there is no place where God has told us not to stay," Mother replied confidently. "This is going to be my life's work. We're not going to move anywhere else."

Standing there on the little knoll, with only the birds and insects as witnesses, Mother Eliza dedicated the land that was to become a lasting monument to God's grace and her persistence in Liberia.

God gave Mother a renewed vigor to face the building of yet another mission. She purchased cutlasses, axes, and other tools, and hired men to cut the brush and dig out the stumps of centuries-old trees. At last a suitable area on the knoll was cleared.

Philip Sota describes the first building: "The walls were made of mud. We put sticks on the ground and tied the sticks together, then put mud on the sticks inside and out, then white chalk on

172

the outside. We covered the roof with a special thatch from the swamp."

Leona George, one of the few girls who had followed the Georges to Plahn, recalls, "We used to work hard while we were opening the mission. Mother would teach us in the mornings, and in the afternoons we worked in the gardens."

Mother knew how essential it was to start growing rice and cassavas immediately. And so she worked in the burning sun, bending from her waist to "scratch rice" like every other Liberian countrywoman.

But the work was too hard for a seventy-two-year-old woman. Otto recalls, "That old lady suffered. Sometimes she walked from six to six from here to Greenville. Sometimes I had to take her water and wash her feet in the night, rubbing them with alcohol, and she would say, 'Son, you have to pray about my going back home.'"

In the Seekon area Mother once again was able to visit native villages where Christ had never been named. In one village when she told the people that she had come from across the sea, one of the old grandmothers placed her hand beside Mother's and said, "Mammy, your hand looks just like my hand. You are my sister. They said long years ago that some of our people here took our brothers away across the water. We have been looking for our brothers to come back home. You are one of our sisters who has come back to us."

"You are one of our sisters who has come back to us."

Mother Eliza couldn't explain to these simple people that she firmly believed that God had allowed her brothers and sisters to be taken away as slaves so that she, like Joseph, could be used to bring salvation to her own people.

In spite of her own painful leg ulcers, Mother traveled to villages with Otto or Petro to dress wounds and treat illnesses with simple medicines. Many were converted in those village ministries. As Otto says, "They believed that God sent this missionary to them to help them, and she wasn't even from their own family!"

By 1952 there were thirty children on the mission. To Mother's great delight, nearly half of them girls. Otto's young sister-in-law, Otheliah, had moved out to ENI with her when the mission house was completed. Mother soon developed a special love for Otheliah. She had a gentle way of ministering to Mother's needs, brushing and plaiting her hair at night and keeping her room (which she still shared with the girls) neat and tidy, the way Mother liked it.

Otheliah would be the first to admit that Mother's material possessions were so few and simple that they were easy to care for. An inventory of Mother's personal belongings reads like this:

    2 or 3 rattan chairs
    a battered suitcase
    a single bed, 2 sheets, 1 pillow
    1 small table
    1 blanket
    2 or 3 dresses and other personal clothing
    1 pair of sandals, 1 pair of high rubber boots
    a bowl, several glasses
    a face pan
    1 tablecloth
    1 calendar on the wall
    1 bamboo mat on the floor
    a big tub over an outside fire
    2 or 3 kerosene lamps or a palm oil lamp in a tin
    a pressing iron for the girls' hair
    a Bible
    writing materials
    a sun helmet

Mother never seemed to have any use for money for herself. One of her boys explained it this way: "She used to spend money as if she didn't need it. We've seen a lot of missionaries, but I'm still wondering if I will ever see another missionary like her. She would pray for the money. She would tell us, 'Let's pray; the mission is out of money' . . . but when the money would come in, you would see the people pour in to her saying, 'Mother, I don't have this' or 'I need that. . . . ' On payday she would be completely broke. Then we would go into another prayer meeting until finally somebody would provide.

> "I'm still wondering if I will ever see another missionary like her."

"She used to give freely no matter what the problem was . . . she didn't care whether you'd committed a crime and needed help or whether you needed the money for religious purposes— she would give the money."

No doubt money was "wasted" through her generous, giving spirit. But that generosity changed the direction of countless lives.

Madie Monroe, named for her benefactor in California, became the matron of the girls' dormitory at ENI. Madie recalls that her father would not allow her to move to ENI when the mission house was ready for occupancy because he had already dowried her to an old man who had several other wives. Madie was only about ten years old at the time, so she was still too young to join her elderly husband.

When Mother learned of this, she called Madie's father to the mission and asked how much dowry he had been paid. It was only $15, but Mother gave him $40 so that the man could not give an argument later that he had been cheated.

It wasn't that Mother didn't concern herself about money. Mr. Miller, a neighbor near Kelton, once met her in Greenville during those early ENI days. She seemed unusually dispirited when he stopped to talk to her. "Oh, Mr. Miller, I came to town because I thought there would be some money, but there is nothing. I'm afraid I'm really down."

Surprised at this unusual admission of defeat from this stout-hearted missionary, Mr. Miller asked, "You mean you're giving up and going back to the States?"

"Oh, no," she retorted, "I'll endure. I'll stay until I've established this mission." And, throwing back her shoulders, she shifted her walking stick and continued up the road, restored from her momentary despondency.

But at seventy-two, the ulcers on her legs would not heal. Mother was forced to walk with a stick, hopping along to keep the weight off her sore leg. She never complained. If people were watching, she tried to ignore the pain and hide her limp.

Someone suggested that she get a jeep to get her back and forth to the mission. Taken with the idea, she wrote to her faithful clubs and churches about the possibility. It was an exciting day when a letter arrived saying that enough funds had been provided through her faithful prayers. With the help of the Lincoln Hatchery in Lincoln, Nebraska, a jeep was on its way. It would be some months yet before it arrived, but Mother talked of nothing else than being able to drive to town for supplies or to take the children to high school in town. The fact that she had never driven anything in her life was of no consequence.

chapter twenty-five

"SON, LET'S PRAY"

*I*n 1944, William Vacanarat Shadrach Tubman became the nineteenth president of the Republic of Liberia. He was to serve the better part of seven terms, bringing unification to the tribal groups and stability to the country.

As a Christian, Tubman was interested in missionary work, and Mother Eliza's contributions in Sinoe soon came to his attention. It was under his administration that Mother's school first received a small monthly stipend.

Having lost the Kelton Mission, the Plahn substation, BIA in Fortesville to the vacillations of overseas mission boards, Mother determined that it would never happen again. Approaching President Tubman, who had given her an audience and sympathetic hearing on several occasions, Mother presented a petition for a grant of land in the Seekon territory where she had begun building ENI mission. In 1952 Tubman granted her 500 acres with the promise that it was hers to use as long as she lived.

Though some of the older workers from Kelton days were faithfully serving with her, Mother was fully aware that none of them was qualified to develop ENI into a far-reaching work. Her heart was still determined to send Augustus overseas. The reports about his progress in Monrovia were encouraging. Though he had completed only five years of schooling in the bush, Mrs. Horton had persuaded him to take the eighth-grade entrance examination, which he had passed with flying colors. After a few weeks it became obvious to the perceptive Mama Horton that even the eighth-grade work was not challenging him. Every quiz he brought home was a near-perfect paper.

Ora wrote a note to her friend in the interior, telling her that she had gone to the dean himself when Gus's shyness deterred him from speaking. The dean immediately recognized that this self-taught young man was brilliant and should be put up another grade. Now in his third year in the high school division of Liberia College, Gus was still at the top of his class.

But Mother was more concerned about his spiritual growth and his burden for his own people. Many of her friends were trying to dissuade her from sending Gus to the USA, reminding her of the disappointment the girls had been.

"He's just a young man, Mother," one friend said. "When he gets over there, he'll meet all kinds of nice American girls, and he won't want to come back and marry some country girl who's not had the education and experiences he's had. He'll just end up staying there. And even if he does come back, would he fit with his people in the bush? Did Maude fit after her American education? No, she felt above them and could never really identify with her own people again. It's just too big a risk, Mother."

She knew that she could trust God to fulfill His will; she just didn't know what it was. Mother knew there was a lot of truth in what her friends were telling her. But she also knew that to provide the leadership necessary to bring the people out of centuries of ignorance and isolation, it would take a man trained beyond what Liberia's present educational system could provide. There was no theological school of higher training in Liberia to challenge Gus's responsive mind and visionary heart.

Mother continued to wrestle with God about this perplexing question. She knew that she could trust God to fulfill His will; she just didn't know what it was.

And so it was that when Gus was called back to the interior for the funeral of his brother, Mother felt she had to spend some time with him. She had been planning to visit the Carpenters in Wedjah. Since she no longer walked those long stretches through the bush alone, it was an ideal time to ask Gus to accompany her. Gus remembers that walk:

> While I was in Shaw for my brother's funeral, Mother sent a message for me to come to the mission, which was ironically now only 20 minutes' walk from my home. She wanted to pray with me and comfort me in my loss.
>
> When I got to ENI I was surprised at the development in such a short time. Though the buildings were still of thatch and mud, they were larger than the ones in Plahn and neatly spaced on either side of the knoll. Mother asked me to teach a few classes while I was there, and I was impressed with the bright students who had come to study at ENI.
>
> Then Mother asked if I would take a journey with her — first to Greenville, where she had some business to do, and then back through Wedjah to visit the Carpenters. She felt responsible to visit their work and encourage them from time to time, and she had not been there for a long while.
>
> That walk with Mother was a turning point in my life. We had hours, just the two of us, to open our hearts and share our innermost needs.
>
> Mother told me of some of the experiences she had in Kelton, things I had never known before. She talked about the people around the mission who had come to know Christ, and other villages she had never been able to visit because of the press of time and work.
>
> Remembering those people, Mother stopped and, putting her hand on my shoulder as we stood in the burning sun, she said, "Son, let's pray." And then she poured her heart out to

the Lord for Maneytown and Murraysville, for the families she knew and the children she had raised, weeping copiously as she prayed.

Then we moved on, Mother leading the way with that tall walking stick which had by now become almost as much of a trademark as her pith helmet. "Son, all these forty years in Africa I've been crying over the lost. Who's going to tell them that Jesus loves them and died for them? Who is going to free them from their ju-ju and devil dancers? Who's going to educate those precious baby girls and keep them from being sold to old men who are just looking for another slave to work in the garden?"

"Son, let's pray." This time she knelt on the trail, her face lifted to the sun, its light reflecting off the thick glasses she had been wearing since her last visit to the States.

Sometimes she asked me to pray. Then again she would stop suddenly in her tracks and say, "You know, son, God has something special in mind for you. He's given you a good mind — yes, a good mind — and He wants you to use it for Him. But, son, don't forget your people here in Seekon, and all those in the interior without Christ. Commit your life to serve Him here among your own people; don't ever disobey His call.

"Son, let's pray . . . . "

And so we walked and talked and stopped and prayed — walk, talk, stop, pray.

On the way back from Lexington, we left at 11:00 in the morning, not arriving at Wedjah until 2:00 a.m. She never seemed to get tired; she never stopped teaching. It was as if she were pouring her life's desires into me until they were pressed down and running over.

As it grew dark, I began to worry about Mother; the road was very rough, with twisted roots reaching out into the path, vines catching us, and branches slapping us across the face.

That night I counted that Mother fell down five times. It looked as if somebody had lifted her feet up from under her as she flew sprawling into the bush. I was frightened, but as I helped pick her up and brush her off, she would quote a verse that had become descriptive of her African walks: "For a just man falleth seven times and riseth up again" [Proverbs 24:16 KJV].

The next morning, when I got out of bed at the Carpenters' place, I was still tired and sore, and I hobbled to the door. I couldn't believe my eyes to find Mother Eliza singing merrily and sweeping the veranda! She was none the worse for wear after her fifteen-mile walk the day before!

In fact, Mother hardly gave her falls another thought—the walk had given her the assurance that Gus was God's man to send overseas for training so he could take over her work. God had spared her life through so many falls and dangers that He could surely keep her for the next seven or eight years while Gus completed his education. What were a few scratches or ulcers and a few more bouts of malaria if in the end God would open up the interior of Liberia for the gospel?

With Gus in his final year of high school, Mother realized that she would have to raise the passage money for Gus to go to America. An idea came to her that she hoped would mean she would not have to burden her clubs with yet another fund-raiser. R. G. Le Tourneau, a Texas millionaire who gave most of his wealth to missions, had begun an ambitious project in the Baffu Bay area, some sixty miles from ENI. She had heard of the heavy equipment he manufactured, and which he brought to clear the forest and develop the land. He even had a ship of his own to bring materials and personnel back and forth. Perhaps he could take Gus to the USA on his ship.

With typical impetuosity, Mother decided to go and see Le Tourneau herself. Taking Otheliah, they walked to the main road and caught a ride on a truck to Greenville.

The stopover in Greenville was especially pleasant. Senator Mitchell, one of her friends who had became a successful politician, had completed his big new house. Elizabeth Mitchell was the principal of the demonstration school in Greenville and wanted to help Mother in her sacrificial ministry. Though she had been sending meals to Mother whenever she learned she was staying in town, Mrs. Mitchell had promised that when her new house was completed, Mother would have her own comfortable "prophet's chamber." When the house was completed, she turned a key over to Mother so that she could come and go without disturbing anyone.

Mrs. Mitchell did complain about one thing, however. "If her girls came down with her, she wouldn't ask for another room. She would sleep on the floor and put them in her bed. I didn't know this until I happened to walk in the room one time and see the two girls in the bed, Mother on the floor. I took her upstairs and gave her my room.

"Mother felt uneasy. 'Daughter, I don't want to embarrass you.'" But Mrs. Mitchell assured her, "I want to do this. You are doing for me what I am not willing to do myself. Why couldn't I have gone out there to work? Just accept this as my contribution."

So for ten years, whenever Mother came into Greenville she had a comfortable room at her disposal and nourishing food prepared.

On this particular day in 1953, Mother and Otheliah woke very early, for they had a twenty-five-mile walk along the beach ahead of them. Mother had not forgotten the heat and the tortuous struggle of her walk some twenty-three years earlier, and she urged Otheliah to get a head start on the sun.

This was Otheliah's baptism into walking on the beach, and she still marvels, "I don't see how she lived through that walk to Monrovia. Even with shoes on, the sand was so hot. Mother wore canvas shoes, and she walked on the edge of the beach where the swell would come to cool her feet."

They arrived at Baffu Bay late Saturday night and bedded down in a friendly village. "Praise God for the wonderful way the natives treat strangers in their midst," Mother would often say. Cleaning themselves up as best they could, they arrived at the mission station in time for church. After the service they were introduced to Le Tourneau, who invited them for dinner.

> "I don't see how she lived through that walk to Monrovia."

But the news was not good. Yes, one ship had come with the equipment and personnel for the project, but it had already gone back, and they were not planning on taking the equipment back, so there was no need of another ship.

Mother understood and thanked Le Tourneau for his invitation for dinner. Getting up from the table, she whispered to Otheliah, "Let's go, daughter. It's time we started for home."

Otheliah still remembers the pain in her feet. "I just felt like crying. I was so tired, and here she was, seventy-four years old and ready to turn right around and walk back again."

But Le Tourneau read Mother's intentions and told her to wait. In a few minutes he had sent word to one of the pilots on the station. Mother and Otheliah were bundled into the plane for the ten-minute flight back to Greenville. When Mother demurred at "embarrassing him," he shook his head. "Nonsense, Mother Eliza—I wouldn't think of letting you walk back that distance again. I'm only sorry I couldn't help you with the young man you want to send overseas."

R. G. Le Tourneau couldn't help Mother. But years later Mother's young man would shoulder the whole responsibility of the churches that had grown out of this ill-fated Baffu Bay project.

chapter twenty-six

THE JEEP AND THE JOURNEY
(1953)

*W*hining in low gear, the jeep inched forward through the underbrush. Further down the path Otto and several of the workmen continued to chop at a stump that was the last obstacle before crossing the creek ahead.

The jeep had arrived at Sinoe port a week before, and with great jubilation Mother and the older boys had gone to collect it. When the ship's crane deposited it on the dock, it seemed as though hundreds of children converged on it, swarming to get a closer look at this strange vehicle. In 1953 a new car was still an oddity in Liberia!

Mother had the foresight to have one of the government drivers come to the dock to show her how to operate the levers and buttons. She never doubted that with a few simple instructions she could drive the jeep safely home.

Of course, there was the problem of getting the jeep to the station once they reached the end of the dirt road. Another twelve miles of uncharted jungle and swamp lay between the road's end and the mission.

As soon as she had heard that the jeep was on its way, Mother began badgering the county to send a crew to build a road to ENI. Roads were still built by the porter system—one shovel of dirt at a time, carried by one man at a time. But though there had been many promises, there was no sign of a road to

ENI yet—and wouldn't be for another fifteen years. Yet Mother was determined to get the jeep to the mission.

She managed to drive the jeep as far as Plahn the first day, where the dirt road ended. No doubt she gave her passengers some unexpected thrills with her erratic steering and sudden spurts, but they took it with the same good humor as she did. She hadn't had so much fun in years! Posing to have her picture taken on the main street with her boys and her friends standing proudly behind the vehicle, she looked as though she had been doing this all her life.

> **She managed to drive the jeep as far as Plahn the first day.**

But out in the jungle the fun evaporated. Revving the engine to a high whine, she charged into a creek whose fast-flowing waters threatened to carry the jeep away. The wheels spun in a mud-hole while Otto and the others rhythmically heaved the vehicle to rock it out of the mud. Horseflies buzzed incessantly around their perspiring bodies, adding to the tortures of heat, mosquitoes, and burns of branches scraping their arms and foreheads as they pushed through the brush.

Although it took almost twenty-four hours to travel the last twelve miles, Mother *did* get the jeep home, to the cheers of the waiting children and their teachers. Otto says that he kept the jeep road open through the brush with his cutlass and shovel for more than a year. No one seems to know where the gasoline came from or how the jeep was maintained without even an amateur mechanic within forty miles.

Mother Eliza could now visit the few villages like Pajibo town along her "jeep road," but she soon realized that this was not a practical venture. The humid climate of Liberia is hard on any kind of machinery, and the people lacked training in mechanics. The maintenance of equipment is a frustration even today.

Mother used the jeep for several years, and then turned it over to one of the boys who was attending high school in Sinoe. Eventually it rolled backward down a hill and was damaged beyond the abilities of the local garage to repair it. At last the jeep was sold to another American missionary who was able to make better use of it.

During this time Mother continued to carry a heavy load of teaching and gardening. But most importantly, she kept writing to her friends in America, to keep them informed about the work. She could never slack off from this, for that communication was the lifeline to her ministry.

Her sister Jenny Belle served as the channel for all funds sent to her. Mother marveled at her careful accounting and faithful reporting. Once when she went home to Texas she saw a jar of Vaseline sitting on a shelf above her bed in her room, and she asked Jenny Belle why she hadn't used it. "Well, sister, it's yours, and you never told me to use it," was the frank reply.

But Mother knew that Jenny Belle worried about her in Africa because of her advanced age, and so Eliza kept a regular stream of cheerful and newsy letters going back to her.

Her friends in the government sometimes worried about her too, and wondered how long she could continue to serve with them. The Minister of the Interior, the now-Senator Harrison Grigsby, may have had this thought in mind when he suggested to President Tubman that it would seem the time had come to decorate Mother Eliza George for her service to God and country.

A surprise program was planned in Greenville; it was to be held in the superintendent's office. Though President Tubman could not come, Vice President Green (at the time, governor of Sinoe County), Senator Harrison Grigsby, and many of the county officials were present. As Senator Grigsby described Mother Eliza's reactions to the whole affair, "Mother is a woman who is never excited about anything. She was calm and cool under almost any situation. But when she heard the citation read, she wept."

> For the many contributions you have made towards the people of Sinoe, particularly the unlettered people of the country, and because of the sacrifices you have undergone . . . I do confer upon Eliza Davis-George the grade of Knight office for the Redemption of Africa.

A bright red, green, and white ribbon, the badge of the order of knighthood, was placed across her chest, looking incongruous against her simple print housedress. The Senator pinned on her shoulder a large silver brooch that bore the motto of the Liberian Republic: THE LOVE OF LIBERTY BROUGHT US HERE.

I do confer upon Eliza Davis-George the grade of Knight office for the Redemption of Africa.

As she stood before her children and the high government officials and friends, bedecked in the nation's finery, for one of the few times in her life Mother was speechless.

But the most rewarding event of that year came later, when she watched the graduating class of the College of Liberia and heard her own Augustus delivering the valedictory speech. It had been a joy to be able to give him a spotless white suit and black bow tie with matching boutonniere for the occasion. After the graduation Mother and Gus had formal portraits taken to commemorate the event.

In California, Madie Monroe had been able to raise enough money for Gus's ticket, and this time, with his graduation diploma laden with honors to present to the consulate, there was no difficulty in obtaining a student visa.

The "Eliza Davis George Club" of faithful African-American women in California provided the affidavit required and guaranteed Gus's support during his stay in the USA. They promised Mother to house and care for him and still continue to help her as best they could. Without their assistance, Gus could never have gone overseas to study.

So Mother now "carried" yet another child back to the USA, and her seventy-four-year-old heart could not deny that she was pinning all her hopes on him.

chapter twenty-seven

ROMANCE IN SAN FRANCISCO

*E*liza hobbled into her room after evening prayers in the dining room. Now that she had several good teachers to help
the children, she no longer had to stay to supervise the studies.
There were always so many letters to answer, and of late she was
finding it hard to see well enough to write. *I probably need a change
of glasses,* she thought. *I'll have to have a checkup next time I go to
Greenville.*

In the past she had to wait for glasses until she got back to
the United States, but now there was an eye doctor affiliated
with the small government hospital in Greenville. The next time
Eliza visited town she went to the hospital on the outskirts of the
community.

The doctor checked first one eye and then the other, taking
far longer than usual. Finally he sat on his high round stool and
folded his hands in front of him. "I'm afraid, Mrs. George, you
need an operation immediately—and it is one we are not
equipped to do here in Liberia."

Eliza froze as the doctor went on. "You have advanced
cataracts, and unless you have that operation within a few
months, you will be totally blind."

Dazed, Eliza stumbled out of the office and back toward the
main street. The doctor was asking the impossible. Very little
money had been coming in lately, and with the large staff and
almost seventy children on the mission, every cent was gone.

Where would she find money for her fare to the USA? Of course she could write and tell her friends about the need, but it would take three or four months for a reply.

Could she borrow the money? Not from anyone in Greenville. They trusted her, but they weren't likely to forward her several hundred dollars for a boat trip to the United States.

Despite her failing eyes, Eliza's lifelong habit of faith was still healthy. Shooting a prayer heavenward, she headed for the post office to pick up the week's mail.

The little post office near the river's edge was a bustle of cheerful talk as friends gathered to wait for the slow-moving clerks to sort the mail. Mother had known the young clerks since they were runny-nosed children hanging around outside the shops on the main street, but she shunned her usual banter with them as she approached to the counter.

> "Son, is there any mail for Mother this morning?"

"Son, is there any mail for Mother this morning?"

The clerk sauntered over to her box and came back empty-handed. "Nothing, Mother, but a new batch has just come in. Do you want me to look through that for you?"

"Yes, be a darling and go see. Mother needs some mail real bad this morning."

It was no surprise to Eliza to open the envelope from a church in Texas and find a check for $600. And it was no surprise for the people in the post office to hear Mother shout "Praise the Lord!" as she hopped out the door and down the street.

When she arrived in Monrovia, there was still one more obstacle to overcome—she needed immediate passage on a ship to the United States. Eliza explained her plans to Ora, who was much more concerned about Mother's eye problem than she was.

"Dearie, the Lord has answered prayer again. The agent said the passenger ship was gone for this month, but there is a cargo ship in the harbor due to sail the day after tomorrow. He asked if I would be willing to take that. I just told him, 'I'll go on anything. I've got to get to the States because they tell me I'm going blind.'"

Friends at the Morning Star Baptist Church of Chicago paid for her operation. For months afterward a grateful Mother would show the little bottle containing her cataracts wherever she went.

Of course she had to see Gus while she was in the United States, so she soon headed for San Francisco. Gus recalls the meeting:

In Mother's usual independent way, she didn't tell me about her coming to the United States, or her serious cataract operation until it was all over. How I praised the Lord that He had spared her eyesight! The operation explained why her letters had been so difficult to read in recent months. I had been wondering if she had suddenly become afflicted with all the usual signs of old age that other people endure. It was a relief to know that it was a reversible symptom and that her sight had been spared.

But I must confess I anticipated Mother's visit with mixed emotions. Though I longed to see her and talk with her, I was not sure she would be happy about my news.

I was now in my first year at Golden Gate Seminary after completing a B.A. at Simpson College. The M.R.E. program would take me two years, and then I would be going back to Liberia. I could hardly wait.

But something unforeseen and unplanned had happened in my life — I was in love.

It all happened so naturally and innocently that neither one of us could say just when it started. Well, I guess you could say it started that morning when I was asked to speak in chapel and tell about my burden for Liberia. I know God spoke through me that morning, for there were many wet eyes in the congregation, and students came up to me for weeks afterward to comment on what they had heard.

But that morning a young lady waited around after chapel until I was free to talk with her to tell me how deeply touched she had been by my message and how she had been praying herself about going to Africa as a missionary. She wondered if there would be some time when I could tell her more about the requirements and conditions and perhaps pray with her about her decision.

We began to meet. The first time was just a general conversation, and we realized that there was much to talk and pray over, so we planned to meet twice a week in one of the upstairs classrooms. We read the Word of God together and began sharing experiences from our Christian life and how God had been leading us.

Before we knew it Donna and I were deeply involved with each other. I guess I really admitted it the first time she was absent from a class we had together, and I could think of nothing else but "Where is she?"

From then on we seemed to spend more and more time together — in the dining hall, study hall. It was just a natural step to begin thinking of marriage and praying for God's guidance in this momentous step.

Realizing it posed some special problems for us, we wanted to seek counsel from someone outside the Southern Baptist leadership at the school. We knew what their attitude toward mixed marriage would be. We wanted someone who would be totally objective — and I guess we really wanted someone who would see the whole thing from our perspective.

Donna had a friend from her hometown of Portland, Oregon, whom she deeply respected, and one weekend we went to *visit Mrs. Schmidt. Listening carefully to our story, this dear lady of God wisely steered us on a neutral course. She said she could see no objection, but that we would have to pray more about it and be willing to face up to the possible problems an interracial marriage might cause. She pointed out that many people would not understand or approve and that we had to take that into consideration.*

So we were back to the beginning. We knew we could go no further with our plans until we had told Mother Eliza. And now here she was, unexpectedly in the United States, and on her way to see me. I was afraid I knew what she was going to say, but somehow hoping against hope that when she met Donna, she would change her mind.

Of course Mother didn't change her mind. She had always been convinced that interracial marriages were not God's plan. A childhood in the segregated American South had given Eliza a disapproving view of such things. Regardless of whether she was right or wrong, Mother had good reasons for not wanting us to marry.

Mother had always been firm with her children, and this was no exception.

Yet as she and Gus and Donna spoke, her heart went out to the two young people. They were so obviously in love, and so desirous of pleasing and serving God. But Mother had always been firm with her children, and this was no exception.

"Children, this is not God's will that you marry each other. Gus has a call from God to return to his own people in the interior of Liberia to take God's message to them. He needs a wife who will understand those people, who knows their customs. You may think, Donna, that you can do those things, but you never will. Those Liberians have hardly ever seen a white woman—you will be strange to them, and they will never understand you. You will become homesick for your own people, and Gus will be caught between pleasing you and obeying God. No, children, Mother cannot give her permission for this marriage."

The young couple assured her they would consider her advice seriously and pray objectively about it, but they did not promise to end their relationship. Mother returned to Liberia wondering if her friends' dire predictions about sending Gus to the USA would come true after all.

chapter twenty-eight

MATCHMAKING MOTHER
(1959–1960)

When Mother returned to ENI, it was to happy news. Jeremiah Lewis, one of her students who had been studying with Gus in Monrovia, had returned to assist Charles Carpenter in the work. With some sixty children in the school and two motherless babies to care for, there never seemed to be enough help.

Mother wrote to a friend in the USA, "I am working on the road. It is a real task, but we mean to get through it some way. We walked one night last week accompanied by two of our boys from four a.m. to four p.m., and how tired we were at the end of our journey! We hope to get the road fixed so that we can drive the jeep and not have to walk so far."

The jeep had been immobilized for some time. Although Mother never again drove it, she held the constant hope that one day she would be on wheels again.

The joy of seeing new converts come to Christ in the villages helped offset the sorrow of losing two babies in 1959. Both infants had been brought in by villagers after their mothers died in childbirth. Tribal belief held that the dead mother became a witch whose spirit traveled around in the night. The villagers wanted nothing to do with a baby who might attract an evil spirit.

It may have been the traumatic losses of the babies that gave birth to Mother's dream of a maternity clinic. First, however, she had to tend to her own house, which was ready to fall around her ears. She had never had a substantial home in Africa in the forty-seven years she had lived there, but her California club was now raising money for such a project. Cement blocks were already being made.

With all the activity and problems of running the mission, Mother's heart continued to ache about Gus's future. She knew it was a difficult decision for him to make. When his letter finally arrived, she couldn't predict what his decision would be.

After Mother left, Donna and I continued to meet, but our talk of marriage and the future had a hollow ring to it. Both of us respected Mother too much to discount what she had said. I think from the beginning we realized that Mother was right. God had a special task for me to do in Africa, and I would be sidetracked with a white American wife who might find life in the African jungle very strange and might eventually want to return home.

Eliza had prayed much about a wife for Gus.

When we finally decided to break off the relationship, Donna transferred to another college. We both felt the situation to be too emotionally taxing, and since I was aiming at graduation in May of 1960, it was not possible for me to transfer to another school without losing credits.

But even while Donna was away she wrote me several very touching letters. She still felt that we could have served the Lord together in Africa.

When Mother returned to the USA for Gus's graduation, she carried in her purse pictures of two of her "daughters" on the mission. Eliza had prayed much about a wife for Gus. She realized that his ministry would be limited unless he married. Tribal people do not consider a man fully mature until he has a wife and child. Gus would need all the credibility he could muster for the task ahead.

The graduation was an exciting time. Mother was filled with a deep sense of pride as she heard over and over what a wonderful contribution her son had made on the campus. Their picture appeared in the school paper together, and an article about Gus appeared in *Christian Life* magazine. Mother met many students who had been part of a weekly prayer meeting for Liberia. It touched her heart to think that these young people cared enough about her people in Africa to pray specifically for ENI's needs.

When the excitement had finally died down and Mother and Gus were alone, she brought up the subject of a wife for him.

"You know, Gustus, that you will need to marry if you are to have the respect of the men in the villages. Also, many of the girls on the mission are young misses now, and it might be a temptation to them if you were unmarried.

"So, I'm suggesting that you choose one of these two girls. I've thought and prayed over this a lot, and I think either one of them would make you a good wife. They are both fine, dedicated Christian girls. They have been with me for quite a few years, and I have trained them to be good housewives and taught them all I know."

She placed two pictures before him on the table. He recognized both of them, but didn't know either girl well. They were both attractive Liberian country girls, and he was sure that Mother had made her choice carefully and with much prayer. Picking up the pictures, he thanked Mother for her care for him, and said he would have to think and pray about it.

I really didn't need very long to think about it. Though I didn't know Otheliah well, I had always admired her sister, Annie. She was married to Otto Klebo. Annie had been the gentlest, meekest girl I'd known, with just the qualities I'd always wanted in a wife. If Otheliah was anything like her sister, she would be just right for me.

And she was beautiful too, with that heart-shaped face and large round eyes that gleamed with a hint of mischief even in the poor picture Mother brought.

I told Mother that Otheliah was my choice and asked her to write to her for me.

Otheliah confesses that she was quite taken by surprise when Mother's letter reached her at Seuhn Academy, where Mother had sent her for her high-school training. She says, "I knew Gus and used to call him Brother Gus when he taught us in Sunday school. He had never shown one bit of interest in me when he had come to ENI to visit.

"Mother told me to let her know whether I would marry Gus, but I didn't know what to say. Before I could answer I got another letter telling me that she was anxiously awaiting my reply. I decided to tell her that if Gus wants to marry me, let him write me himself."

I wasn't surprised at Otheliah's answer. I remembered her with just that kind of spunk, and I was glad for that. After my years in America I would find it hard to get used to a girl who just agreed to everything I said, with never an idea of her own. So I sat down to compose one of the most important letters of my life. Even to this day I can just about remember it word for word.

Dear Otheliah,

Having discussed with Mother Eliza about the work and about the girl I should marry, Mother talked so highly about you that I decided to get married to you.

I've known you on the mission and I've been impressed with the life of your sister. So when Mother shared with me about the kind of girl you are, I fell deeply in love with you, and I would like to get married to you.

By the grace of God I plan to come home this year, and I would like to get married right away. May God bless you.

Yours truly,

Augustus

When I left for Monrovia in November 1960, I carried in my pocket a well-worn letter of acceptance from the girl who had agreed to be my wife, and a beautiful picture which I showed to everyone who would look at it.

When I arrived in Monrovia, Otheliah was waiting for me at the Hortons, looking shy and a bit ill-at-ease, but even more beautiful than her picture.

chapter twenty-nine

"SON, TAKE IT!"

(1961)

H *ow many times have letters brought news that shattered my life?* Eliza thought as she slowly put Gus's letter down on the table in front of her. It was January 1961. She was home once again with Jenny Belle in the familiar little clapboard house.

When Gus's letter arrived that morning, she eagerly tore it open. She hadn't heard from him since he had returned to Liberia. Was he happy with her choice of Otheliah for him? What were their wedding plans? How soon would he be going out to ENI?

She had read with pride the article about him in *Christian Life* magazine. Granted, it had sounded a bit presumptuous: "After six years in the USA for education, Marwieh this month becomes director of the Elizabeth Native Interior Mission in Liberia."

Perhaps that was a bit premature, Eliza thought. She intended to retain her leadership for a few years yet—at least until Augustus had been well indoctrinated and properly introduced.

But once again her dreams were shattered. She couldn't blame Gus. He had been placed in a difficult position. She read the disturbing paragraph once again:

Dr. Tolbert asked me to come and see him as soon as I arrived in Monrovia to discuss our relationship with the Southern Baptists. He took me in his limousine to visit

Ricks Institute, the Liberian Baptist school on the outskirts of Monrovia. You know it, don't you, Mother? On the way there he asked me to teach at Ricks, since they are desperate for qualified staff. I was really taken aback, for you know how we planned for me to return to ENI. I told him I would need two weeks to think about it. What should I do, Mother?

Eliza could well understand Gus's predicament. Not only was Dr. William Tolbert the vice president of Liberia, but he was the president of the Liberian Baptist Convention, and Ricks was a Convention school. Naturally he would want a man of Gus's qualifications to teach at this important institution. How naive of her to think that she could keep this gifted and highly educated young man for her own little work out in the bush!

"I'm eighty-two years old and the burden is getting too heavy for me to carry."

Instinctively she began praying aloud. Jenny Belle was used to hearing her sister's open conversations with her heavenly Father.

> *"Dear Lord, You're the one who brought Gustus out of the interior to study at my mission. And now I need him to take over for me, Lord. I'm eighty-two years old and the burden is getting too heavy for me to carry. But dear Jesus, if you need Gustus at Ricks more, then I know you can take care of ENI too. Bless Gustus today. Guide and direct and protect the entire mission. Provide for Gustus as he takes on this great responsibility. May the angels who encamp about those who love and fear you encamp around him. Amen."*

Gus had written Eliza a number of times during the previous two years about his desire to have the Southern Baptist Convention send missionaries to Liberia. While earning his M.R.E. at

Golden Gate Seminary he became familiar with their leadership and mission program. He believed that God could use them to alleviate the great spiritual and material needs in Liberia.

At first the leaders of the Baptist mission board refused. There were already three other Baptist groups working in Liberia, and furthermore the Southern Baptists were planning to enter new fields in Angola and Mozambique.

But Gus would not take no for an answer. He had written Mother about the prayer groups he had organized and which now met on campus almost daily to ask God to change the minds of the con-

> **"Now the sun of my life is sinking on the goingdown side."**

vention leaders. He encouraged Mother to add her voice to Gus's pleas by writing Dr. H. Cornell Goerner, secretary for Africa of the Southern Baptist Mission Board. She wrote:

> "I have with and without support tried to keep alive the spark of missionary work until Augustus returned. Now the sun of my life is sinking on the going-down side, and I humbly appeal to you and your foreign mission board of the Southern Baptist Convention to share with the humble missionary endeavor in Sinoe County, Liberia, where Augustus is going, and strengthen it before it dies."

Suddenly God began to intervene. The governments of Angola and Mozambique refused the Southern Baptist's application to enter their countries. Vice President Tolbert heard about Gus's request and added his own appeal for help. Finally, the leaders of the Southern Baptist Mission Board found themselves on the same plane with Dr. Tolbert when they flew to the Baptist World Alliance in Brazil. Surely this was not mere coincidence but divine intervention.

So it was that when Gus returned to Liberia arrangements had been made for the Southern Baptists to send missionaries to work with the Liberian Baptist Convention. Gus was certain that ENI would benefit from this new relationship.

But Gus had never dreamed that this alliance might involve his own commitment. His first response was to say no. He had been preparing to return to his own people in the bush for six years. All the time in America he had prayed fervently that he might not die like Sammy Morris, that great black missionary who passed away before he could ever return to Liberia.

Eliza knew what she must do. Even though Gus had asked the advice of missionaries in Monrovia (they had all urged him to accept the appointment), she knew he would not make a decision until she heard from her. Reaching for her handbag and cane, she pulled herself wearily to her feet.

"Jenny Belle," she called to her sister in the kitchen, "I'm going over to the post office. I won't be gone long."

Her telegram was to the point: SON, TAKE IT.

She had one more task to complete on this day of January 28, 1961. Now that she had heard from Gustus, she must answer the letter of his friend, Mr. Finley.

Gus had written several months earlier: "Allen Finley, whom I met several years ago through International Students, has been taking me to churches where I could tell about the work at ENI. In fact, he has offered to arrange a deputation tour to help me raise funds for my passage back to Liberia."

The previous December, Eliza had received a letter from Allen Finley:

Dear Mother Eliza:

I am writing to you because of our mutual interest in our dear brother Augustus Marwieh. I am the general direc-tor of Christian Nationals Evangelism Commission, the organization that helped him on his trip cross-country. The Lord richly blessed him and gave him some funds to help get him on his way back to Liberia, and we hope this will also mean some future support.

CNEC has helped native workers for twenty years. We have a wonderful board of godly men from across the nation who have sought to do this type of work, and the Lord has blessed it. We are now supporting about 105 native evangelists in Malaysia, Thailand, Singapore, and Hong Kong . . . and now we are also seeking to help Gus . . . . We are set up so that we do not maintain control over these men, but we seek to share with them in the work God has given them to do.

We are already set up in relation to Augustus, with funds going to him and toward the support of his work . . . . CNEC needs to release its funds to a mission, and certainly our desire is to release all we can raise for Brother Augustus to the ENI mission, but I would appreciate it if you would explain or send us some information on how this mission is set up.

Eliza didn't know just what this new organization would be willing to do for ENI now that Gustus wouldn't be working there. But she owed Mr. Finley some kind of answer. She decided not to write about this latest development just yet.

Dear Mr. Finley,

Long ago you wrote me . . . . I was waiting to hear from Augustus . . . . I received a letter from him this week stating that he will marry on the 29th of this month. That is tomorrow. We pray God's blessing upon him and his choice for a companion in life. The Lord blessed me to humbly share a part in training both of them.

Now with regards to our work. It has been one of the struggles by faith in God that has helped us through his friends. I appreciate your interest in Augustus especially now, for this is the beginning of his new field of many difficulties.

Sixteen years ago the Liberian government gave me 500 acres of land for missionary purposes, and we have not done very much cultivating of the land so as to make the work self-supporting along the lines of agriculture. We do not have substantial buildings, but have erected country houses, have taught school on the main mission and out-stations, and have sent out native missionary workers.

It may be of interest to write that the 20th of this month was my 82nd birthday.

The next day, 100 miles away in Monrovia, the Hortons gave Otheliah and Gus a beautiful wedding in the St. Simon Baptist Church, where Mother had worshiped so many times. Dr. Horton performed the ceremony, and the reception was held at their home, up the street from the church. Gus recalls the day:

We had a Western wedding and then took a Western honeymoon—something unheard of in the bush. A cottage was made available on the premises of ELWA, the Sudan Interior Mission radio station, whose beautiful campus stretches for almost a mile along the palmlined beaches of the Atlantic Ocean.

I can say with a pure conscience before God that I never knew any other woman. I did not know Otheliah until our honeymoon. This was a "pure fact"—even though I did not get married until I was 33 years old. But God miraculously kept me. I spent time on my knees struggling; only God's miracle kept me. There were times when I was absolutely as weak as water, but by God's grace I was able.

chapter thirty

THE GREAT WHITE ELEPHANT
(1961)

*Y*oung man, I'll have you know I've been in this country
longer than you are old! God sent me here, and if He sent
me here, nothing can stop me." Seeing the startled look on the
face of the young Liberian customs officer, Mother gave him a
warm smile, adding, "Now you be a dear and just do what you
have to."

Later, at the Hortons, Mother related the incident to Ora as
the two old friends sat up late in the night catching up on all the
news. "I guess I should have gotten a visa back in the States, but
once I had enough for my flight, the only thing I could think of
was to get back here." Then with a hearty chuckle she added,
"But you know, dearie, they gave me my visa anyway. I just
charmed them! Now tell me all about Gus's wedding."

On the surface Mother had not changed much. Her gray hair
swept smoothly back from her face. Although her cheeks had
hollowed out to accentuate her determined chin, her skin
remained remarkably unwrinkled for her eighty-two years. She
still held herself erect, but her ulcerated leg forced her to resort
to hopping when she wanted to move quickly.

Mother still gave the impression that she was very much in
charge of any situation. But closer scrutiny would reveal an
underlying weariness. Gus's appointment to Ricks had hit her
harder than she anticipated. She had fully expected to return to

find him at ENI, carrying the heavy burden of the work, relieving her of the many decisions and daily cares of her growing mission family. She confessed to feeling in spirit like the song composed by the slaves: "Keep inching along like the poor inchworm; we'll get home by and by."

Besides the usual care of the school and churches, more and more motherless babies were being brought to her. Several died on the mission during that year of 1961.

In a letter to one of her friends she said, "When I wrote you last our motherless mission baby was seriously ill. She now sleeps in the arms of Jesus. It is not an easy task to rear babies in this country, but we tried our best for this little one."

She began planning a clinic to care for mothers and babies.

And when she announced the joyful news of the arrival of Gus and Otheliah's little son in the hospital in Monrovia, she added, "Where we are, the children share their part in sightseeing when a woman gives birth in their village."

In spite of her weariness, she began planning a clinic to care for mothers and babies.

Though Mother didn't fully comprehend the implications, she began receiving assistance from two organizations during that year which would eventually be the means of growth and expansion far beyond her fondest dreams. Shortly after arriving back in Liberia she received the first regular monthly gift of fifty dollars from Christian Nationals Evangelism Commission. The money had been given for Gus and his work, but since he was receiving a salary from Ricks, he asked that it be sent to Mother Eliza at ENI.

In response to the first gift, Mother wrote to Allen Finley:

Thanks much for your abiding interest. The gift sent by your board goes a long way to help.... Struggling for many years by faith with only God through a few friends here and there, you can imagine how much your assistance is appreciated.

Thanks for your prayers. Saving souls and bringing up the moral side and character-building can by no means be considered an easy task. Gus and I have always been one in the Lord along this line.

Just one week ago Josiah, our assistant teacher to Charles on the mission, triumphantly passed to the other side. Noiselessly he did his living best in everything he was called upon to do. We miss him.

We have 85 day students. Before going to the USA we had 65 boarders, but the responsibility is too great now.

One week ago the Lord blessed us with six lovely converts. They went with Him in baptism.

Chiefs in the interior are begging us to send missionaries to teach their children. So many children have never seen a schoolroom, and many grown-ups further on have not yet heard the sweet story of Jesus and His never-dying love. Pray much for us . . . our cares are many.

Four of our boys are attending school at the beach; they are writing me of their needs. Thirteen churches (each with a national worker) plus 25 boarding children, 85 day pupils, and one motherless baby present the need for Bibles, songbooks, and schoolbooks. There is also a $300 debt. Jesus says, "Owe no man."

It may be of interest to write that a white couple will soon come to Sinoe to help us. Praise the Lord for His goodness. This couple we believe too has the Christlike spirit.

It is now after one a.m. At early morn after prayer three of us are to begin our tramp to Greenville.

Yours trusting, Mother Eliza George

Shortly after, Mother visited one of her newly established national churches, using the same old ankle express that had served her for so many years. It was an eight-hour walk through a pouring rain, swollen rivers, and over foot logs. But she still felt the urgent need to keep in touch with her "missionary children" and to encourage them in their work.

> She still felt the urgent need to keep in touch with her "missionary children"

At the church she was faced with yet another request for a school—more than a hundred church children had no such opportunity. The burden was almost more than she could bear. She had to find a way to start another school.

Back in Monrovia, Gus and Otheliah had settled into the fine house provided by the Institute; Gus even had a car. He was happy to provide his lovely young wife with the comforts of the city—electricity, shopping convenience, running water—all the things she would never have enjoyed out at ENI.

But he was deeply disturbed at the thought of Mother struggling alone out there on the mission while he worked comfortably in the city. Rev. Poe, the first Southern Baptist missionary sent to Liberia under the arrangements made after Gus's request for additional help, was the principal of Ricks. Noting Gus's discomfort over the turn of events, Poe urged the Southern Baptists to send someone to help Mother Eliza "or we will lose him."

By September of 1961, John and Betty Carpenter arrived to help Mother. John and Gus flew to Greenville together and then drove to Plahn to meet with Mother and the church leaders. Gus captured the excitement of his first visit home when he wrote:

> My dear Friends,
>   A very moving, dramatic scene was made on the 21st of October when I visited my tribal people for the first time

since my return from the USA. People from all over the surrounding and distant villages traveled miles to come to see
me and Rev. Carpenter, an American missionary whom
God has sent to help us carry on the labor of love among
my people. The sight was one of the rarest I have ever
seen. The people display all kinds of emotions, each
according to his peculiar emotional constitution. Some
sang, some danced, while others cried profusely. Sometimes they hugged me, sometimes they picked me up, and
sometimes some tried to carry me on their backs. When I
saw so many people, most of whom have no relationship to
me except by tribe, going so wild about me, I was over-
powered by the thought of how my father, my mother, my
brother, or my uncle would have felt if they were living.

The time of reunion with my people was one of the
happiest moments in my life. It was incredible to think that
I, who less than nineteen years ago left home as a boy,
almost completely naked, could return to my people with
a Master's degree, shoes on my feet, a tie on my neck, and
dressed in a suit. I left home believing in superstitions and
witchcrafts and returned as an ordained minister with a
gospel message. Can you imagine that?

When the Carpenters moved out to Greenville later that
year, they were the first white missionaries to work with Mother
Eliza. John Carpenter had come primarily to assist with the
development of the church work, relieving Mother of that
responsibility. But she soon encouraged him to handle her funds
as well. He became, in a sense, her business manager. Mother
jokingly referred to him as "the great white elephant." For the
first time in her ministry she could send people to someone else
when they came for help.

Rev. Carpenter admits that Mother was good-hearted to a fault. "She just didn't realize that people were taking advantage of her. I put her on a budget and made available only a certain amount of money to be spent on materials. When her helpers came down to get supplies, for the first time in her years in Africa she was able to operate in the black, and that was simply because I defended her from those who would take advantage of her."

But Rev. Carpenter was quick to praise Mother Eliza for her overwhelming love for people. "No one could ever question Mother Eliza's love. And that love caused her to go to any extent to try to provide an education opportunity for them.

"No one could ever question Mother Eliza's love."

"Interestingly, before we got to Liberia I had a vision of her being very brittle, cantankerous, overbearing, and demanding, and I had a fear of having difficulty in working with her. When we got there, we found her just the opposite.

"One thing stands out . . . she was so jovial, so deeply spiritual. She could go through the longest periods of fasting and praying . . . she had a sense of humor about everything."

Rev. Carpenter felt that the African church leaders whom Mother had raised were good men but had little training. "I never had any quarrel with Mother on her theology or biblical interpretation," he explained. "She approached the Scriptures from a devotional standpoint. She bathed herself in the Scriptures."

But the men needed more systematic training in the Word of God, and this Carpenter began to do.

Now instead of Gus feeling sorry for Mother, Mother began to feel sorry for Gus. During her first year back at ENI, Mother sent eight mission children to stay with the Marwiehs in Monrovia. One was a mission baby whose uncle had threatened to steal and sell her. Gus was struggling, so Mother wrote to CNEC:

I wonder if Gus has more on his toes than he can kick off his heels. He is now acting principal as well as teaching at Ricks. He has eleven mouths to feed, including his wife and children. I took $13.50 of the $50 sent by CNEC and sent Dessie to Gus. I should be sending something to help Gus but do not have it. He, like myself, accepts more upon him than he is able to do. I still believe the $50 should go to help Gus and his wife.

In August, Mother spent some time in the Greenville hospital. The ulcer on her leg had been irritated by a cat's scratch, and the infection was eating right to the bone. For the rest of her life it continued to trouble her. Several times doctors threatened to amputate the foot, but Mother wouldn't hear of it. There was still no road the last twelve miles through the jungle to ENI, and she was determined to keep walking as long as God gave her strength.

She was determined to keep walking as long as God gave her strength.

When Gus came to help John Carpenter with a pastors' Bible school at ENI his heart was encouraged to see what a load had been lifted from Mother's shoulders. There were now sixteen pastors, and even though there were no substantial buildings, the churches were growing.

Gus also brought some exciting news for Mother—at least *he* thought it was exciting.

"The Southern Baptists have decided to make a 30-minute television program about your work at ENI, Mother. They want you to come back to Monrovia with us to film it there, since they can't get their equipment out here to ENI."

But Mother was aghast. "No, son, I don't think I should do that. The Lord has given us this work, and He doesn't want us to take any glory for it. That would be wrong for me to put myself forward like that."

But Gus and Rev. Carpenter wouldn't rest until they had convinced Mother that the TV program would not be glorifying her, but would promote her beloved work. When she finally acquiesced, she became as excited as they were about the prospects. The TV crew loved her for her acting ability and her boundless wit. Narrated in the United States after the filming was complete, Mother was not aware how prestigious a commentator would introduce her to the American public.

> Hello, Americans—I'm Paul Harvey . . . my newscast is over for today, but I have another story . . . the struggle to conquer the American frontier. . . . That struggle was repeated on a new frontier—Liberia—by other Americans, by Negroes like Mother Eliza George. . . .
>
> As the Liberian nation looks to a sure and prosperous future, Mother Eliza George looks at the two men, Augustus and John . . . and knows that the work she began fifty years ago will continue to grow.

By the time the program was televised in the Southern Baptists' series, "The Answer," in March of 1963, Mother had returned to the USA with yet another baby, Keturah. Struggling with wet diapers, bottles, and a fussy infant, she took a third motherless child on the long journey to the States to be placed in a Christian home. She held hidden hope that one of them would return to their own people to serve God in Liberia, but none of them ever did.

Once again Mother Eliza was back on the deputation trail. She left Keturah with a family in Illinois who adopted her, and then Mother began in earnest representing the needs at ENI. Her goal before the end of the year was to raise enough money to erect three buildings on the campus—one for the boys, a chapel, and a building for motherless babies.

Gus asked his friend, Allen Finley, to help Mother make arrangements for meetings, but it would be August before CNEC was able to catch up with Mother's busy schedule. In a quick note explaining what she had been doing, she wrote:

"I had my last meeting in Chicago on the 21st of August. Then I ran down to Toccoa and Marietta, Georgia, on the 23rd and returned to Chicago on the 27th."

Not only was CNEC trying to contact her, but Sherwood Wirt was eager to interview her for an article for *Decision* magazine. Mother traveled to the Minneapolis headquarters of the Billy Graham Association and spent several hours with editor Wirt. Her story appeared in the February 1964 issue of *Decision*. The article closed with her impassioned appeal for help:

"We need nurses over there. We need medical missionaries. We need houses for motherless babies. I am in Chicago right now seeking funds, but I yearn to get back to Liberia so badly. It is a great country, and it needs Christ. The Africans see what we are doing, and they look up at the moon and sun and stars and say, 'Big man up yonder.' But they don't know Him! So many have a zeal, but not according to knowledge. Pray for them! And pray that God will raise up more young American Negro Christians to minister to their brethren in the land of their fathers."

After years of deputation in black American churches Mother concluded, "Our people on this side have such a limited vision of the work to be done over there."

So she threw herself even more enthusiastically into meetings, speaking in every black church that would give her opportunity. She planned to return to Africa early in 1964. But tragedy struck.

Sister Ellen, who had been living with Jenny Belle for many years, suddenly became ill, and in a few days was gone. Sorrowful, Eliza returned to Tyler to share in the family's grief, little realizing that Ellen's death would mark the end of her permanent ministry in Africa. Though she would return to Africa several times in the next nine years, she would remain the head of ENI in name only.

Deep down, Eliza knew that this is what she wanted. After all, she had prayed for a replacement for years. Nevertheless, it pained her to realize that her leadership was no longer needed.

chapter thirty-one

THE MANTLE
FALLS TO GUS

I felt so sorry for Mother. After Ellen died she stayed another six months with Jenny Belle, trying to help her adjust to the great loss. Jenny had always been close to Mother; in fact, had faithfully forwarded funds and channeled receipts to Mother's donors for many years. Mother could not have carried on without her, especially after the National Baptists retired her.

So now, of course, she felt responsible for taking care of Jenny Belle. They were the only two of the eleven Davis children still living.

Cecelia was living in Austin, just 30 minutes' drive away, and she did what she could to keep an eye on Jenny. But Cecelia had three children and was holding down a job, so it wasn't easy to run back and forth frequently.

By May, Mother felt Jenny was strong enough to be left alone, and so she returned to Africa. I think she felt she was losing her grip on the work and needed to get back.

But she had been in Africa only a month when she received an urgent message to return to Texas. Jenny Belle had had a serious nervous breakdown. And so for the third time in one month my 87-year-old spiritual mother flew halfway around the world.

Though Charles Carpenter was doing a fine job of carrying on the school at ENI, I was becoming more and more exercised about the spiritual darkness among the tribal people in the interior of Liberia. The coastal areas had been evangelized for many years; yet I could still remember how my mother, Nyonobe, had invited strangers from Grand Gedeh to stop and rest while she prepared a meal for them. As a boy I would hang around listening to the men tell their tales of war; I was intrigued by their strange-sounding dialect and different ways.

Yet, as far as I knew, no one had gone back to those people with the gospel. They were dying in darkness while I had been so richly blessed in Christ.

Though these thoughts kept nagging at me, it wasn't until a night in January 1965, that the issue came to a head. I couldn't sleep, but lay tossing and turning far into the night. Even with the electric fan clattering in the open window, the air was thick and muggy — a typical Liberian night, and I had known many of them.

A picture of an old man kept passing across my mind — the old man I had met on the trail as I walked back to ENI last time. The trails were overgrown, barely visible in the thick jungle bush. It was a long, arduous walk to the clearing, where a dozen thatched huts were clustered.

The old man had been lying outside the door of his hut at the edge of the village, a ragged, mud-colored blanket covering his skeletal frame. When he opened his eyes as I approached, they were like two luminous holes sunk deep into his head. I had not intended to stop here; I had hoped to meet the chief and his counselors and arrange a gathering of the whole village as soon as the people came in from their fields.

But something compelled me to stop and kneel beside the obviously suffering figure. "Old father," I said gently, putting my hand on the frail shoulder, "I've come to tell you of the great Father above who loves you."

The luminous eyes burned into mine as I shared Christ and His healing touch, inwardly wondering if my words were penetrating. When I finished praying, the old man called out, "Woman, come here."

An equally frail-looking woman appeared in the doorway of the hut. "Get the box!"

Without a word she disappeared into the hut and returned with a battered tin chest. Almost reverently the old man opened the lid and began taking out strange and exotic articles: a polished stone, a greasy woven pouch from which a pungent odor emanated, some gaudy beads, and a grotesque wooden image.

Taken aback, I recognized the tools of trade of a powerful witch doctor, and I wondered whether the old man was going to use them to try to drive me and my message of God away.

But the old man, handling the artifacts one by one, replacing them in the box almost lovingly, suddenly turned the chest upside down on the ground and commanded, "Woman, burn them. The God of heaven this man has told me about doesn't need my magic."

Over and over, the transformed face of the old man came to my mind as I lay on my sweat-stained bed, and I knew what God was saying: "Gus, it's time to go back to your people in the jungle. You've had that vision for many years, and now is my time. There are thousands like that old man who need to hear of me, and you are the one to go and tell them."

I knew the day had come, but did I still want to go? I looked over at Otheliah, asleep at my side. She deserved the nice home here at the Institute, with electricity and servants. And ruefully I had to admit that the chauffeur-driven car was a luxury I would miss. In the jungle one walked!

As I lay there I rationalized: these city young people were the future leaders of Liberia. It was important that they have dedicated Christian teachers. There were few enough of those in Liberia.

Perhaps I was just being sentimental. People with lesser education and gifts could certainly work among those primitive village people who still lived on the same subsistence level they had a hundred years ago. Perhaps I could raise money to hire pastors (but there are no pastors out there). Perhaps I could send literature out to the villages (but they can't read). Or perhaps I could find someone else with the vision for those tribal people (but I've given you the vision, Gus).

Would Otheliah agree to go back?

The first thing in the morning I told her of my long struggle and decision and I asked her, "Will you return to ENI with me, Otheliah? It won't be easy — you know how isolated and backward it is."

But Mother Eliza had chosen my wife well; she knew the caliber of the woman God had given me. Otheliah answered without a moment's hesitation, "If God is leading us to go, let's go."

There was still one more obstacle: Dr. William Tolbert, then vice president, had asked me to join the staff, and I felt I should receive his permission to resign. That very morning I excused myself from my classes and went to his office. He had often told me to come see him at any time; even though he was an extremely busy man, he wanted me to feel free to call upon him. That morning he was just on his way out to inspect a government project, and he invited me along. Riding in the back of his limousine, the window between us and the driver pulled shut for privacy, I poured out my heart to him.

I don't think he had ever really heard the story of my background and what I owed to Mother Eliza. But when I finished telling him about my decision, he answered as a true Christian, "If God is leading you, then who am I to stand between you and the Lord?"

I was jubilant and began putting things in motion to speed my release. There was just one little matter I hadn't quite figured out. Who would support me and my family?

The obvious answer to me was the Southern Baptists. They had come to Liberia at my instigation. I was working at Ricks, which had become their special project. One of their missionaries was in charge of Mother's churches. It seemed so logical.

But when I broached the subject, I was jolted to reality. Southern Baptist policy did not allow the mission to support a national worker; that was the responsibility of the churches. I was told to think it through very carefully. "You have a family . . . those children of yours have a future. Where will you get support if you leave Ricks? The Bible tells us to count the cost before we make a move. Don't jeopardize your family for a foolish dream."

But my mind was made up. With or without their support I would return to ENI. I made arrangements to leave Ricks in September. I knew that God had taken care of Mother Eliza all these years, and I could certainly trust Him to take care of me.

Just before leaving Monrovia the thought came to me that I ought to write Allen Finley at CNEC. Perhaps they would consider helping me expand the work at ENI. Before there was time for a response from him Otheliah and I were back at ENI.

What a welcome! The jubilation of my first return with Charles Carpenter was nothing compared to the love poured out to me and my family when my tribe learned that I had come home to stay. From surrounding villages miles away groups came in day after day bringing gifts of rice, chickens, goats, cassavas. We received so many chickens that we had to build a special house to keep them. For a month the celebrations continued, and we had enough food to keep our family for the rest of the year. That was God's first answer to our prayer for provision for my family.

Then came a letter from Allen Finley saying that he and two of his board members would be coming out to Liberia to visit ENI, and that if they were satisfied with what they saw, they would consider assisting the work to meet our current needs.

But there were problems too. My dear friend John Carpenter and I had to come to the parting of the ways. It was a friendly parting, for we loved each other in the Lord. But he wasn't happy about my working independently of the Southern Baptists at ENI, and I think he was a little concerned that I expected to take over the leadership of Mother's churches as well.

I didn't want that. John was doing a fine job training the pastors, and there were now 27 churches in the Eliza George Baptist Association. So we agreed that the churches would stay with the Liberian Baptists (with whom the Southern Baptists were working) and that I would take charge of the ENI mission. Of course, I planned to plant new churches, but wasn't there the whole unreached interior to work in?

Just about that time Mother came back to Liberia for a visit. She could stay only a few months because she did not dare leave Jenny for long. She still carried on a busy deputation schedule, raising her own travel funds as well as funds for the mission.

For the first time I sensed a little strain between Mother and me. I didn't realize it until several years later, but she feared two giants were taking over her work, and that I was contributing to their takeover.

ENI had so long been Mother's full responsibility. She had given her life to see it grow, had suffered physical pain and hunger, had wept copious tears in prayer, had fasted days on end — all to bring salvation and education to the "native children," as she so endearingly called them.

Now her age limited her leadership, and my return to ENI (the very thing she had been praying about for years) was taking her beloved work out of her control. Though her mind was alert, it seemed that she was more easily influenced by people around her.

Nevertheless, we had some good times while she was there, and she was able to meet Mr. Brewer, one of the CNEC board members, who had stayed longer than Mr. Finley and Elton Fox, another CNEC board member. When Mr. Brewer left, she was convinced (at least for the time being) of the wisdom of working with CNEC.

While Mr. Finley was here a wonderful thing happened. Delegates of the Shaw tribe came with a letter signed by the paramount chiefs, clan chiefs, and elders of Seekon and Tarjuozon chiefdoms, stating:

> Whereas the ENI Mission is dedicated to the spread of the gospel of the Lord Jesus Christ and to the education and training of our children and to the development of the resources of the land for the benefit of our people and to the bringing of medical help to our districts, we do hereby attest that we have given to the ENI mission for their permanent use and development 8000 acres of land, beginning from Samunien of Plandabalebo Town and Pebleh Town, Nyarn, to the southeast.

The letter was signed with the crosses and signatures of sixteen village elders. Visions of cocoa and coffee plantations, enabling ENI to become self-sufficient, danced in my head. And when CNEC wrote some months later to say they had agreed to send $350 a month to support the running costs of ENI, I was confident that Mother's work was finally on a solid financial foundation.

Before many months had passed, I took a 150-mile hike into the interior, carrying the light of the gospel to those unreached people. They responded with such a movement of God that we saw 30 churches established and leaders appointed in each one. Mother's dreams for evangelizing Liberia were at last coming true.

chapter thirty-two

A HAMMOCK RIDE
INTO THE DARKNESS
(1969)

*E*liza disdained traveling by hammock. She felt so helpless swinging in the air, suspended between four men picking their way along the jungle trail.

"Why, what if they trip over a stump or step on a snake?" she used to argue with her husband. "They'd spill me right out on the ground."

The plain truth was that Eliza was just too independent to place herself into someone else's hands. But this morning, as the file of porters wound slowly through the jungle, Mother was glad she had given in. She would be ninety in a few months, and though she could still walk many miles, this trip to Gbaizon would have been more than her old body could take.

Mother's body was aged, but she did not believe in pampering herself. Her body had been tempered to fine steel as she pushed it to the limits of its endurance. It was because of her marvelous resilience that Gus had felt free to ask her along on this arduous journey into Gbaizon.

Nearly three years earlier, when Gus had first returned to ENI, the Krahn tribe had sent a representation to the mission, begging him to visit their area. As soon as he was able to free himself from the responsibilities at ENI, he and a group of pas-

224

tors had taken the 150-mile hike through the Gbaizon area, where people had never heard the gospel.

Mother wept when Gus told her the story. How well she remembered her first visits to the villages around Kelton—her warm welcome, the eagerness with which the villagers heard her story, and the shame she felt when they asked her, "Mammy, how long you people know about this Jesus?"

The Krahns in the Gbaizon area had responded to the gospel with such wholehearted abandon that thirty congregations sprang up during Gus's month-long trip.

Now the women of the tribe had sent a message to ENI: "Come and bring some women to preach to us; you have sent men but never a woman. We want to learn more about God's Word too and how to change our ways."

It did not seem strange to Eliza that the Krahn women wanted to hear from a woman. After all, their lives were so different from those of their husbands. So little real communication between the sexes existed in tribal life. Each had a distinct role to play. How could a man understand the tensions of two or three wives living together? The jealousies? The fears? Accusations of witchcraft or curses in pregnancy?

Being a woman had never limited Eliza's ambitions or dreams for her ministry.

Being a woman had never limited Eliza's ambitions or dreams for her ministry. She always knew that God intended her to use every ability, strength, and opportunity He had given her. She gave deference to ministers and was glad to have them preach and baptize. But most of the time there were no men to preach or teach, to counsel or advise, to discipline, or even to farm and build in the places where God had called Mother.

In spite of her strength and take-charge tendencies, Mother retained an old-world charm that men admired and respected.

One of her friends observed, "Men took orders from her—even Liberian men—when they wouldn't take that from any other woman."

The traveling party grew to about fifty people as it moved slowly up hill and down, through swamps and across rivers. Gus had asked his friends, the De La Haye's at Radio ELWA, to come along on this missionary journey. Besides the SIM missionaries and their friends, there was Gus and his wife and four children (the youngest, Sophie, just a babe in arms), and Mother Eliza. When the Gbaizon church learned that the team was on its way, they sent a delegation of forty people to meet them at the end of the road to help carry their supplies and accompany them back on the three-day walk into the interior.

To Mother the excursion was a miracle, though she had depended on miracles all her life. During these fifty-four years in Africa, her heart's desire had been to go further into the interior to preach to lost souls who had never heard the gospel. That was why she had moved Kelton farther away from Lexington than the townspeople wanted her to. That was why she wouldn't move the mission to Monrovia, as the Baptists had wanted her to. That was why she kept sending her children out as missionaries at great personal sacrifice—and some said to the detriment of her own work at the mission. She had never lost her vision for the country people, who had so long been excluded from the good things of earth and heaven.

She had depended on miracles all her life.

And so she drank in the joyful, rhythmic singing of the porters, and the cheers and ululations as they entered each village along the way. To sleep again in the chief's hut as a privileged and honored guest in the village brought back memories of her first treks, when she and Susie had worked together at BIA.

Wherever they stopped in the evenings the villagers gathered in their simple church shelters, decorated with palm fronds and wildflowers. Though the people all sat on logs or bamboo poles, the honored guests were given chairs or benches at the front of the church. Out of their simple fare they brought gifts of love—chickens, fruit, rice, even a billy goat.

There were many speeches, but the people listened most attentively when the "God-woman" whom they had heard so much about got up to speak.

"Children, Jesus bore the cross for you. I've seen missionaries following Jesus bearing His cross. Every one of them could have been comfortable at home.

> **"If I had a thousand lives, I'd give them all to God for Africa."**

"Africa gave birth to black people. I'm not ashamed of being black. My mother said to me, 'Liza, if I was a black man, I would go back to Africa.' When I was in my mother's womb, she said she had a longing to come to Africa. It came out in me. I love Africa. If I had a thousand lives, I'd give them all to God for Africa.

"Pray for our people in America. They are busy accumulating things, which are just for time and not for eternity."

When Eliza challenged her listeners to pray, it was not an idle cliche. She believed in two basic solutions to all her problems and had followed this simple plan all her life: every situation and every need was immediately taken to her heavenly Father in prayer. While other people slept, Eliza prayed; when crises called for fast decisions, Eliza prayed; and when things got tougher than usual, she fasted. During one very difficult period at the mission Mother fasted for eleven days, then got up from her bed and walked to Greenville for supplies.

Eliza loved the jungle, and she never feared its treachery. Even on this three-day journey into Gbaizon she was undaunted by the heat and the obstacles. The porters carried her though twenty-six swamps and eighteen streams. But she would just as happily have gotten down from her hammock and forded them by ankle express if they would have allowed it. At one point a big tree had been felled to span the distance across a wide river. The porters could not balance the hammock across the log, so Mother sat astride the "bridge" and worked her way across herself.

Eliza was to visit Africa one more time, in 1972, when Dr. William Tolbert, now president of Liberia, personally decorated her "for distinguished and sacrificial services . . . for more than fifty long years as a missionary, teacher, mother, and friend . . .

Mother knew that Gus was God's man for ENI.

who struggled for the redemption of man's sick soul at countless cost . . . a faithful servant in the Master's vineyard."

But nothing would give her greater joy than this journey into Gbaizon, to know that the gospel had spread to the very heart of Liberia, and to see her spiritual son leading the way.

There were difficult times in the later years as Gus and Mother struggled over the direction of the work. It is never easy to turn your life's work over to someone younger, even if it is your own son, and to allow him to bring changes that seem unwise or revolutionary. But in her heart Mother knew that Gus was God's man for ENI.

At sundown on the third day the procession arrived at its destination. Sophie De La Haye, the SIM missionary who traveled with the party, vividly described what transpired:

> With hundreds arriving from all the surrounding villages, the town was turned upside down. The church was packed to overflowing, not only with the 600 women who had invited us women to come, but also with their husbands and children, who came along too.
>
> No one present will ever forget the service on the second evening. We visitors, seated on the platform along with Gus, Mother Eliza, Otheliah, and several of the leaders, sensed an undercurrent of excitement.
>
> At a certain point in the meeting Gus turned to Mother Eliza, seated beside him, and said, 'Mother, my people are in darkness. Can you give me light to share with them?' Then we saw that they had arranged this between them. Mother Eliza took a candle out of her pocket, lit it, and then lit the candle Gus was holding in his hand. Turning to the pastor beside him, Philip Pajibo, he lit his.
>
> Then we noticed that everyone had candles. The light quickly spread from one to another — to the choir, then down the rows of men, women, and children seated on mud benches and in the aisles. A little girl sitting on one of the open windows held her lit candle high . . . hundreds of candles burning brightly revealed smiling, joyful faces. What a sight — I'll never forget it!

"It's wonderful to think that one little candle I've lit — Gus — has already lit so many others."

Tears were streaming down Mother Eliza's cheeks as she realized what her little light had done, just like the chorus she had so often taught her children—"This Little Light of Mine."

Philip turned to Mother to say, "We're thankful to you tonight that you didn't hide your light under a bed."

Then Mother turned to the crowd and began to speak. "Many times I've been lost in the night in the jungle, when only one little candle could have shown me the way. It's wonderful to think that one little candle I've lit—Gus—has already lit so many others. How I praise the Lord for these lights! I'll go back home to the States talking about them."

Turning to Gus, she said, "Son, I'm so glad that when we sent you away to study you did not lose your vision for your own people. Praise God that you have returned to help your people in Liberia."

Smiling into his eyes, Mother took his hand and pressed it warmly as their love for each other and for their Lord bound them in an even deeper understanding of what God had done for them. There would still be struggles in the years ahead, but at this solemn moment Mother knew that she had turned the torch over to him once and for all. He would carry it bravely into the darkness.

chapter thirty-three

"100 IS LONG ENOUGH"

Mother Eliza, undeterred by the advancing years, returned to Texas to continue her deputation schedule. At one of her last meetings in Dallas, at ninety-nine years of age, she spoke to a banquet of young blacks. Challenging them to mission work, she dramatically threw her cane down on the platform and strutted across the stage unaided as if to say, "See, if I can still do it, you can."

Several months later she broke her hip. Her adopted daughter, Cecelia, moved her and Jenny Belle to a nursing home in Tyler so the two could be closer to her. Cecelia visited Mother and Aunt Jenny every day, frequently bringing a bag of candy, which Mother loved so much. She remained alert and loved by everyone in the home.

On January 20, 1979, Mother celebrated her hundredth birthday. She was able to leave the nursing home and attend a gala festivity at the local Baptist church, even giving a speech.

Twelve thousand miles away, in Greenville, Liberia, hundreds of Mother's children had gathered for an even greater centennial celebration. A colorful parade wound through the city streets, led by a band and people carrying banners.

ONCE YOU KNOW HER,
YOU'LL NEVER FORGET HER—
MOTHER ELIZA GEORGE,
THE GREAT MISSIONARY OF THIS CENTURY

Another read:

GREAT DAUGHTER OF AMERICA
GREAT DESCENDANT OF AFRICA
GREAT SAINT AND MISSIONARY MOTHER

And a third:

HER LIFE WAS THE BEST COMMENTARY
OF THE BIBLE WE HAVE EVER READ—
THE LIFE OF ELIZA DAVIS-GEORGE

Speech after speech followed as those whose lives she had touched shared in the celebration: Newspaper George, former commissioner of Tarjuoville; Philip Pajibo, head of the Gbaizon church; Moses Pajibo, principal of Sinoe High School; Gus Marwieh, director of ENI; Benjamin Jlay, private secretary to the president of Liberia; Daniel Saywiah, magistrate of Juarzon; Jacob Slah principal of CNEC High School; Edward Kofi, commissioner of Sanquin Municipality; Tom Bestman, teacher; and many others.

The Gbaizon choir was there too, all the way from the interior to add their voices to the celebration.

A message was read from Dr. William Tolbert, and a third decoration was conferred upon Mother Eliza George:

In consideration of sacrificial and selfless services rendered which are deserving of honor, merit, and distinction, I do hereby confer upon

Eliza Davis-George

the grade of *Dame Grand Commander* in the most venerable order of Knighthood of the pioneers of the Republic of Liberia.

But of all the speeches and honors, Mother would have been most delighted to hear of the development of the work she had begun.

- Baptist Industrial Academy—now a Liberian Baptist boarding school
- National Baptist Mission (the new Kelton)—ten churches (in association with National Baptist Mission Board, USA)
- Liberian Baptists in Sinoe—Eliza Davis George Pastors' Training School—fifty churches (with Southern Baptist help)
- ENI mission—five primary schools, one high school, one technical school (under Gus Marwieh's leadership and CNEC assistance)
- Independent Churches of Africa—100 churches (under Gus's leadership and CNEC assistance)

Perhaps Mother now knows of these honors and the growth of her work, but she did not learn of it while in Texas. A few days after her hundredth birthday she was rushed to the hospital with pneumonia. Cecelia stayed at her side, but she realized that Mother had decided that "100 is long enough."

On March 8, 1979, Mother Eliza Davis-George went home to the heaven she had told so many people about during her long life.

BORN TO LOSE, BOUND TO WIN

$\mathcal{T}$he little candle passed on to Gus back in Gbaizon continued to flicker as Mother Eliza's spiritual son, Gus
Marwieh, received her mantle. Gus and Othelia continued to
expand the work at ENI—building substantial buildings for the
high school and later a technical school, training hundreds of
rural young people.

In those early years, Gus recalls, "I was crushed by the
thought that if we did not get the Gospel of our Lord Jesus
Christ to rural Africans before they died, then having suffered so
wretchedly in this life, they would die without Christ and would
suffer again throughout eternity."

Even before Mother Eliza's death Gus had started the Africa
College of Evangelism, training students not only to pastor
churches but to move into the interior as missionaries among
unreached people.

In 1982 Gus and his family moved into Monrovia, the capi-
tal of Liberia. With only ten percent of the population of the city
attending church Gus realized that the mission field had moved
into the city. While pastors trained by him and Mother Eliza
continued to serve in the 120 churches, now united as AICA, Gus
began several ministries in Monrovia with the help of Partners

International (formerly CNEC). There he began moving in the high circles of government and business, using his influence to share his faith, and encouraging the leaders of the country to help the rural Liberians.

On a visit to the USA he met Dr. Schuller of the Crystal Cathedral who captured Gus's vision for his people, and sponsored Gus to appear on a weekly TV program in Monrovia to preach the Gospel to the nation. Suddenly Gus became a national figure as everyone with access to TV, with only one channel, saw his program.

Mother Eliza must have seen the entrepreneurial spirit of her adopted son. She would not have been surprised to learn of the prison ministry he founded; the work among children, the missionary training school, and the technical high school at ENI. Just like Mother Eliza, Gus was ever optimistic and seldom discouraged, even though the constant humidity rusted machinery; students without any mechanical background damaged equipment; and there were never enough funds to fulfill his dreams.

In another ministry, Christian Institute of Personal Evangelism, many of Mother Eliza's former students trained indigenous missionaries. With training in agro-technology these missionaries fanned out into the countryside to establish small agro-tech schools and planted thirty-five churches.

Just as Gus received the approval and cooperation of the government to build an institution to train government teachers in agro-tech education, war broke out. On December 24, 1989, a civil war broke out; it destroyed the infrastructure of the country, killed thousands of Liberians, and drove many thousands into refugee camps. In April 1990, Gus and Othelia were flown out of the country for their own safety, and could not return for ten years. Today there is nothing left of the work at ENI, though many of the churches continued even through the seven years of civil war. Most of Mother Eliza's "children" are dead—either through natural causes or as casualties of the war.

During those years Gus earned his doctorate in missions at the Reformed Theological Seminary in Mississippi. But his heart was ever in Liberia, and though he could not return because of the civil war, God stirred him to help his people in other ways. In 1992 Gus established AHEAD (Agency for Holistic Evangelism and Development) with the help of Christians in America.

Dr. Romeo Horton, founder of the Bank of Liberia and son of Mother Eliza's friends, the Hortons, served as a member of the board. In 1997 AHEAD established a college program to train high school graduates who had sat for years without schooling in the refugee camp. The school has trained a thousand young people and adults in theology and evangelism, agriculture, building construction, community health, accountancy, business management, journalism, and cottage industry. It has a church-planting department to train indigenous missionaries and evangelists.

Even in his seventies, Gus continued to dream dreams for his beloved people of Liberia. He drew up an agreement with the University of Winneba in Ghana to train specialist teachers. Since the refugee camp is just a few miles from the university, professors can commute to the camp to train the students.

"Our objective for training the Liberian refugees is to equip them so they are qualified to help in the evangelization and reconstruction of our war-ravaged nation," Gus declares.

Still ringing in Gus's ears is the challenge Mother Eliza gave him on their heart-to-heart walk so many years ago.

> *You know son, God has something special in mind for you. He's given you a good mind and He wants you to use it for Him. But son, don't forget your people here in Shaw and Seekon and all those in the interior without Christ. Commit your life to serve Him here among your own people; don't ever disobey His call.*

NOTE TO THE READER

The publisher invites you to share your response to the message of this book by writing Discovery House Publishers, Box 3566, Grand Rapids, MI 49501, USA. For information about other Discovery House books, music, or videos, contact us at the same address or call 1-800-653-8333. Find us on the Internet at http://www.dhp.org/ or send e-mail to books@dhp.org.